With Different Eyes
Imke Braselmann

Do You See What Eye See? - Volume 2
A book with creative pictures that will open your eyes to the little things.

With Different Eyes
Do You See What Eye See? - Vol.2

© 2018 Imke Braselmann
1. edition
All rights reserved

More information and products at:
www.mitanderenaugen.eu

More books on amazon and other online and retail shops

With Different Eyes

There is so much to see if you just open your eyes and look around.

Everywhere you look, in scuffs and stains, on trees and stones, on the street and in forests, you can find things that look like faces or animals.

This phenomenon is called Pareidolia. Not everyone can see these creatures, but with a pair of googly eyes at the right spot, the creatures come to life.

Try it out and see the world "with different eyes"!

The next time when you go outside,
look for the creatures, `cause they hide.

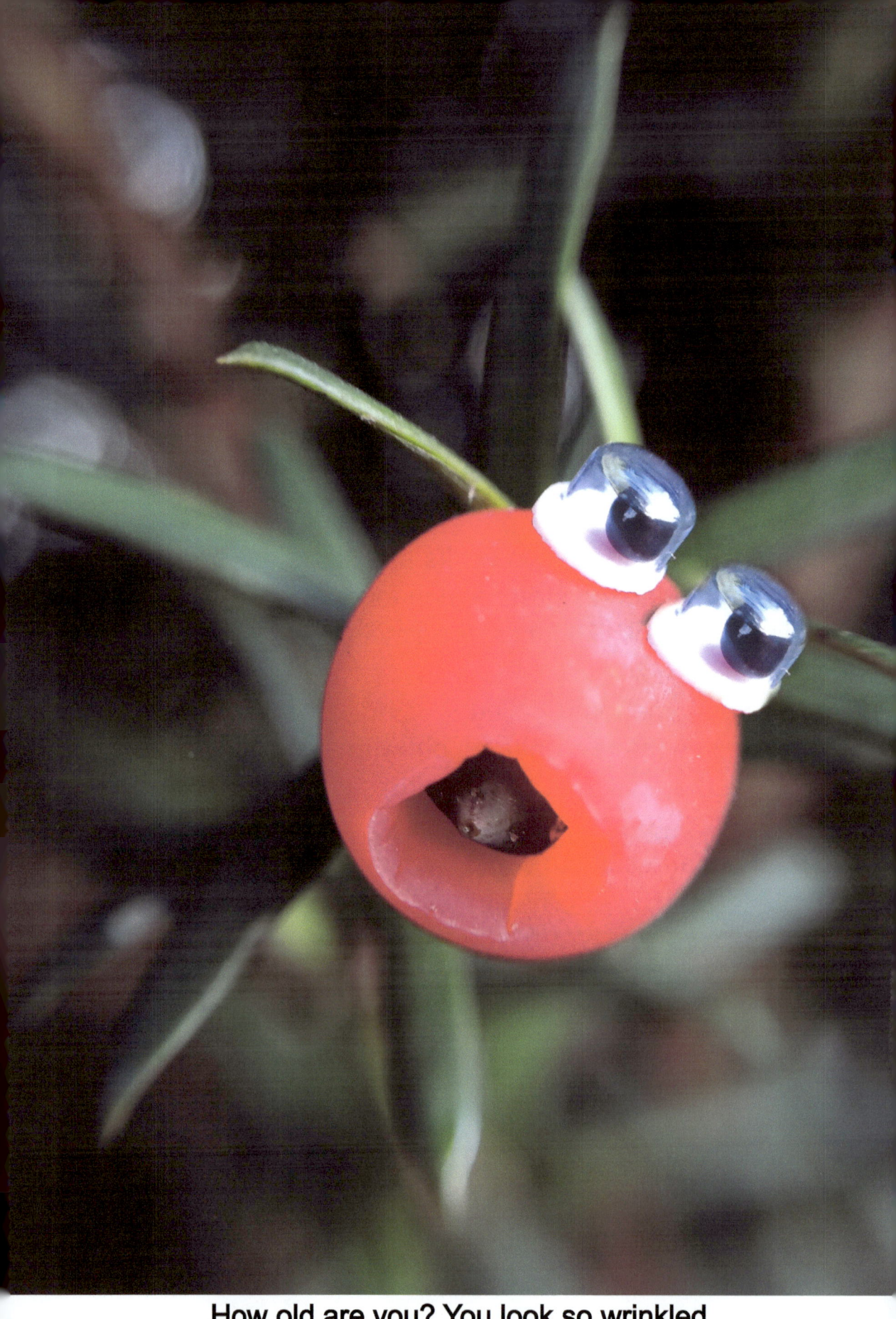
How old are you? You look so wrinkled.

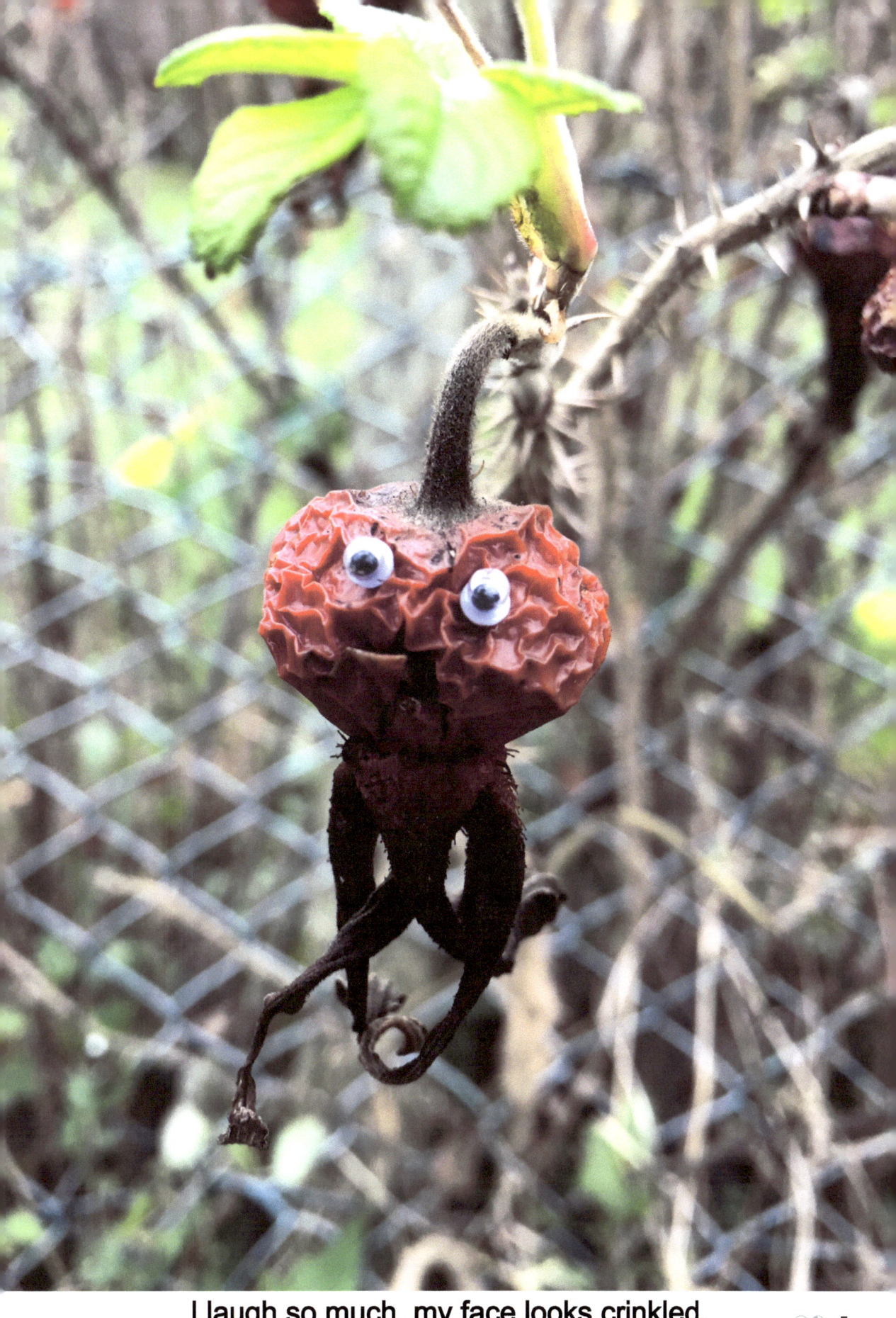
I laugh so much, my face looks crinkled.

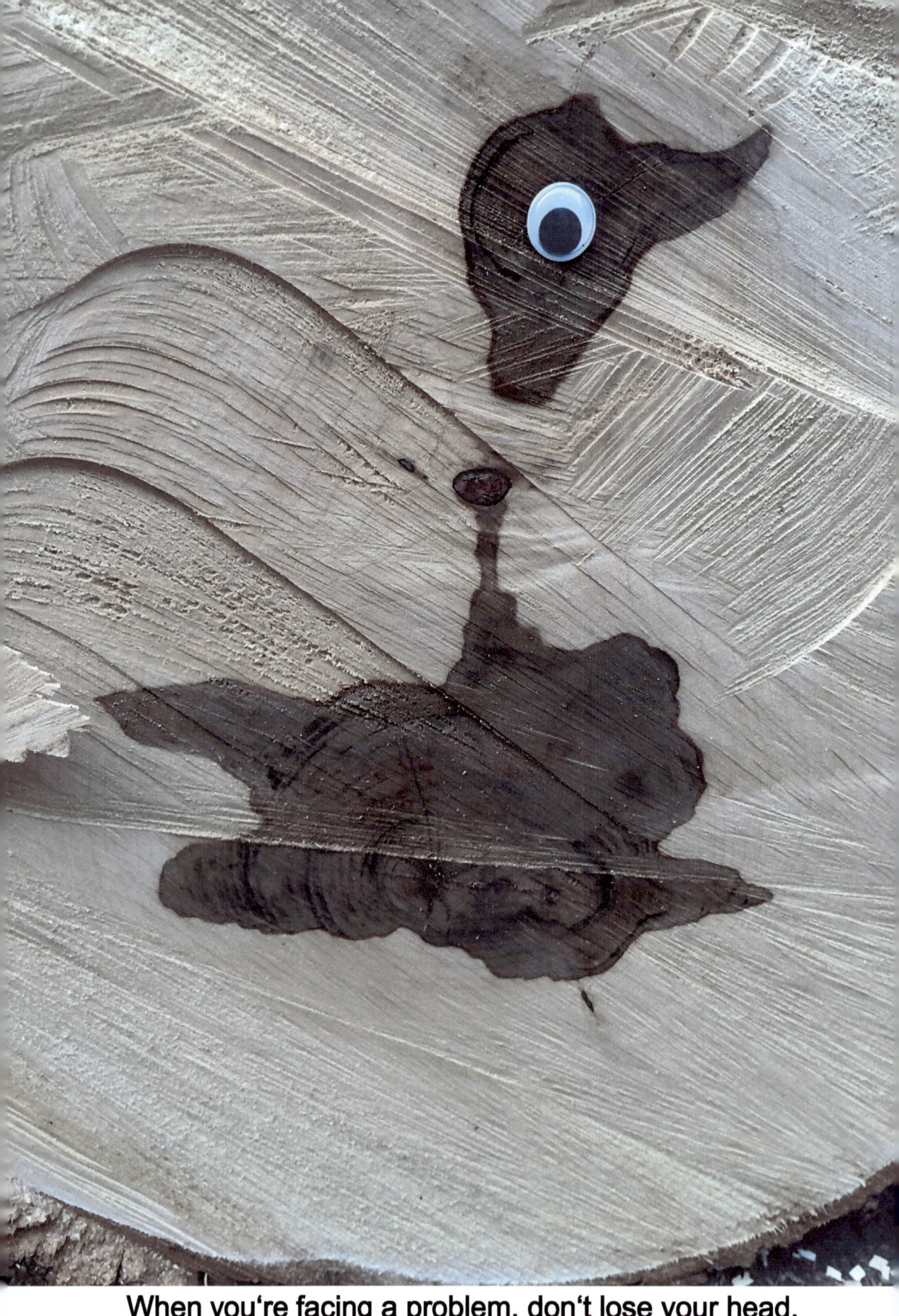

When you're facing a problem, don't lose your head.

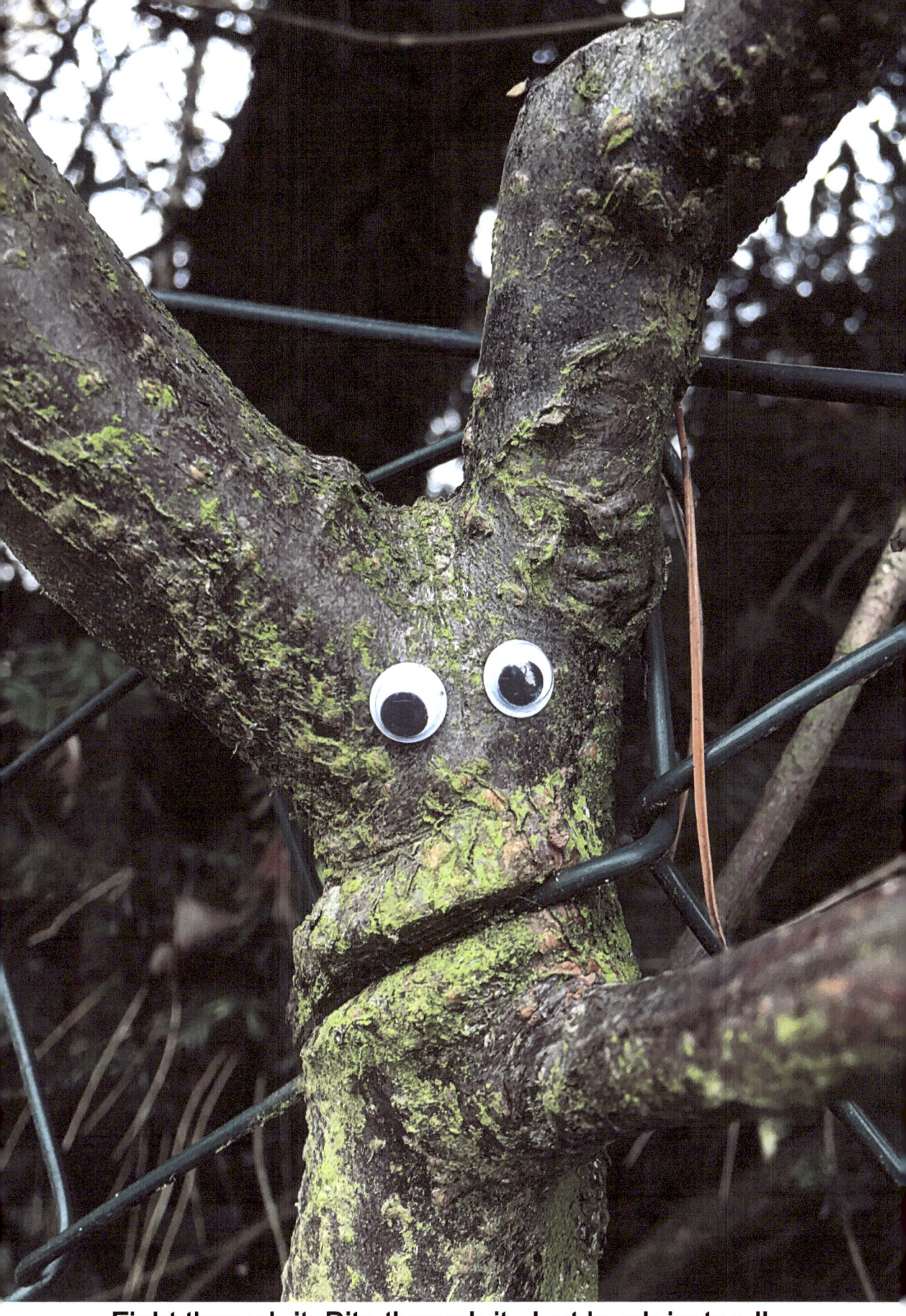
Fight through it. Bite through it. Just laugh instead!

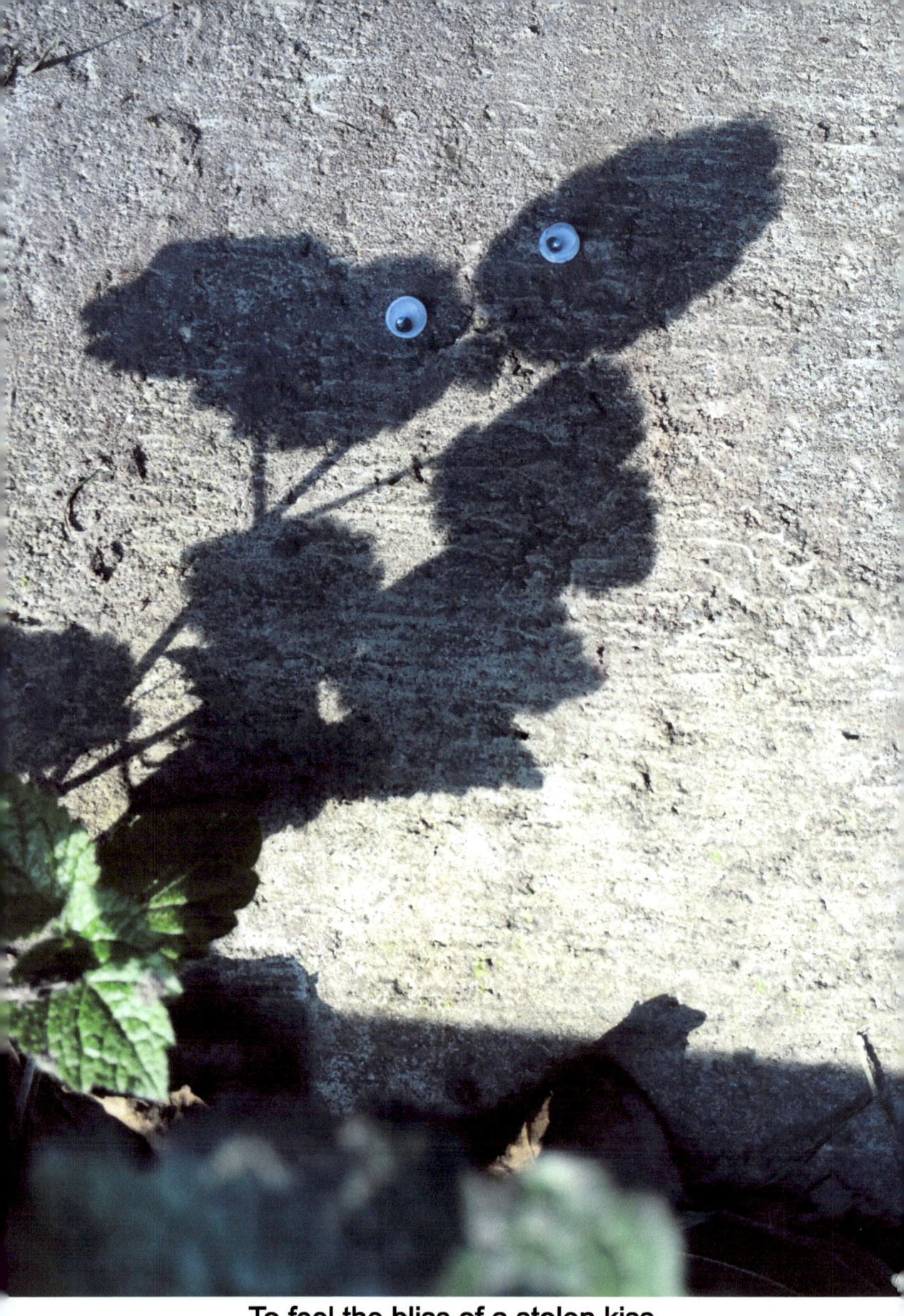
To feel the bliss of a stolen kiss...

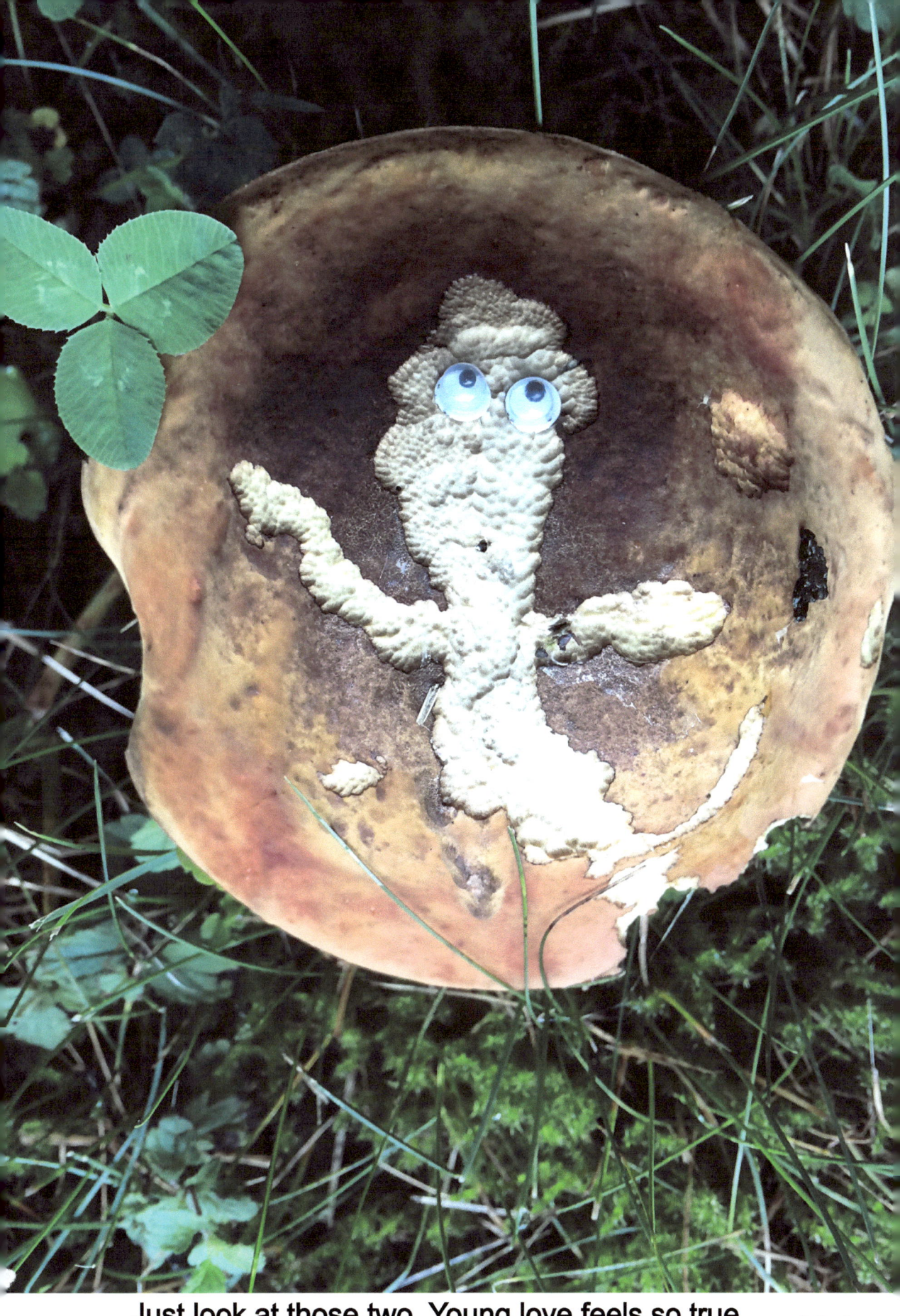

Just look at those two. Young love feels so true.

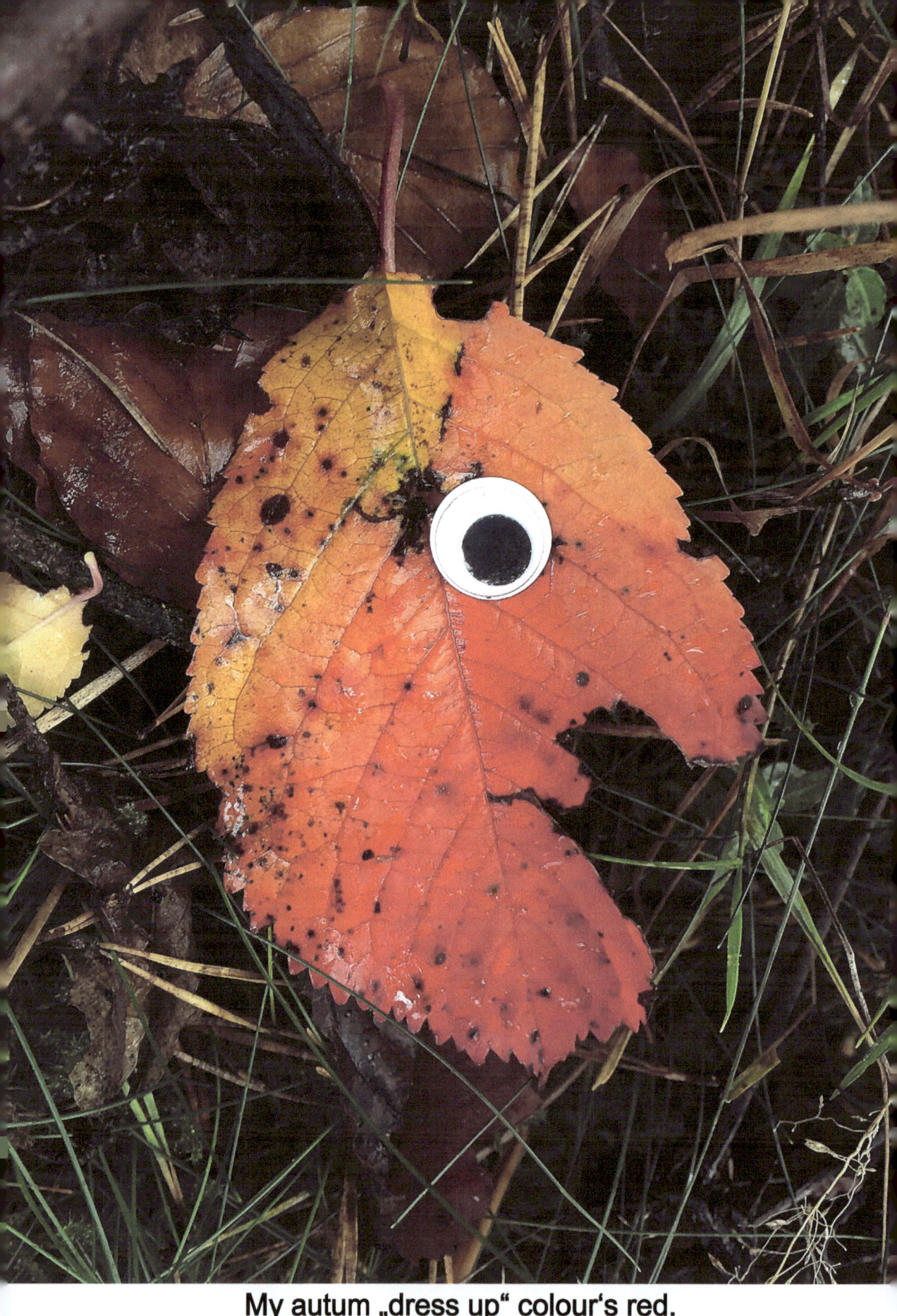

My autum „dress up" colour's red.

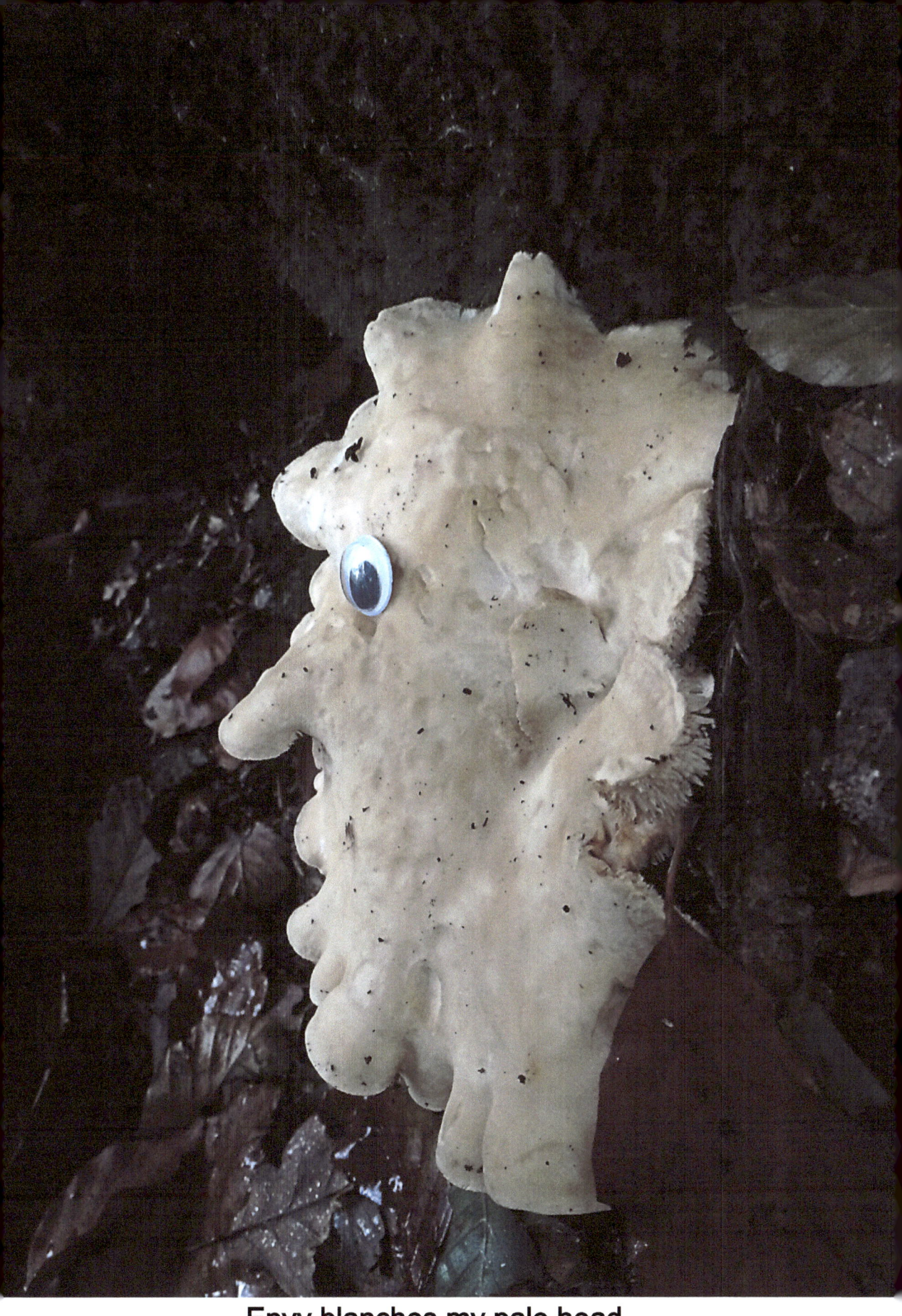

Envy blanches my pale head.

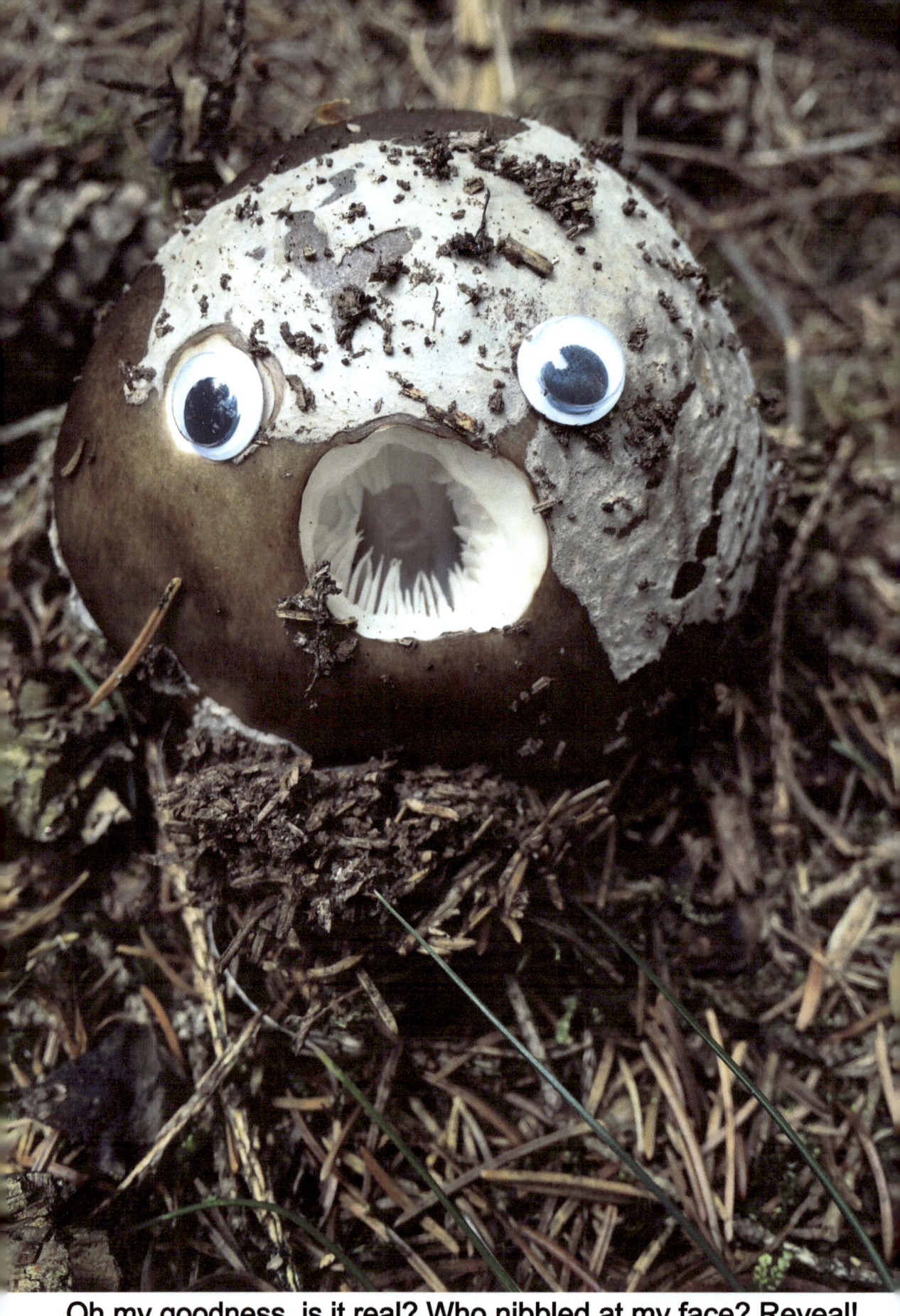

Oh my goodness, is it real? Who nibbled at my face? Reveal!

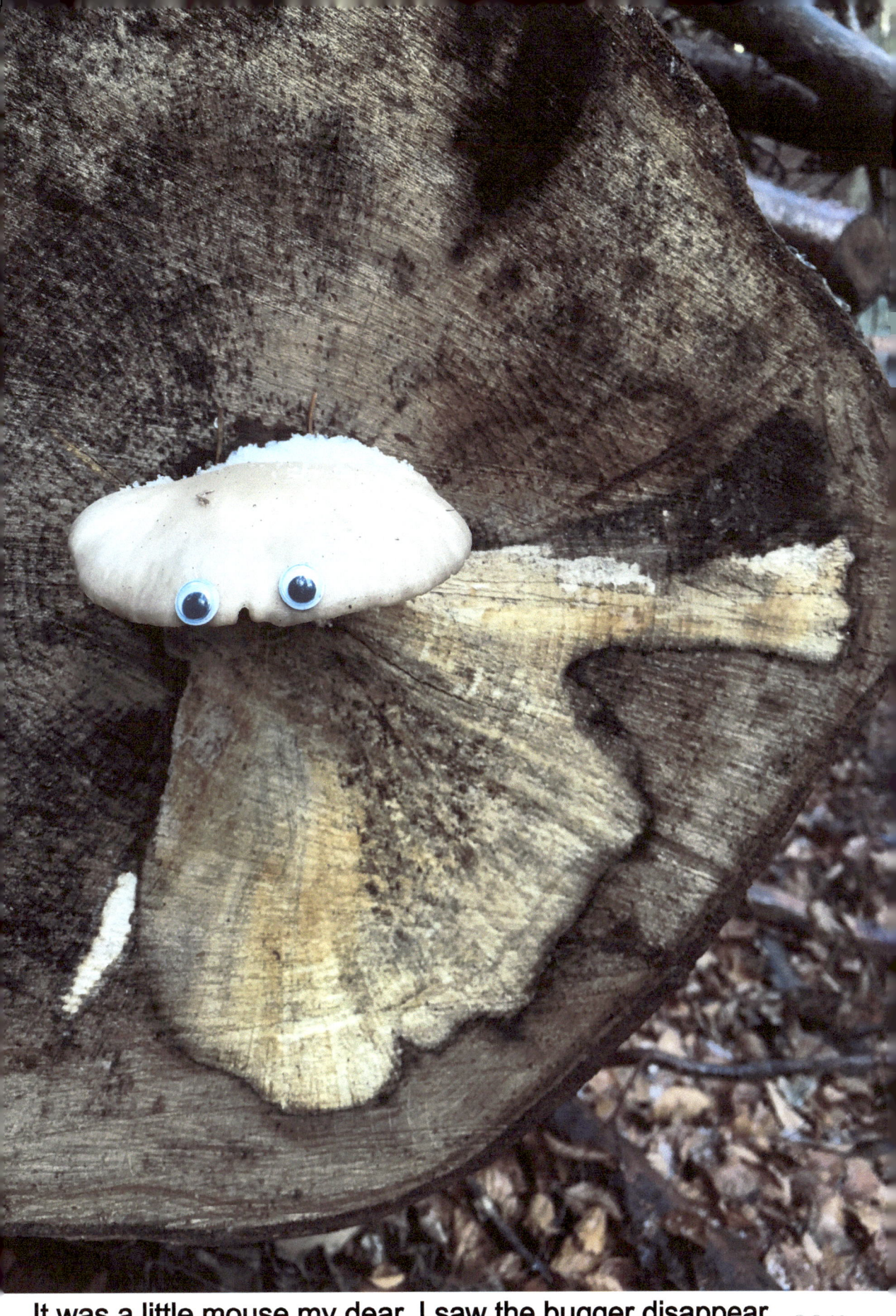

It was a little mouse my dear. I saw the bugger disappear.

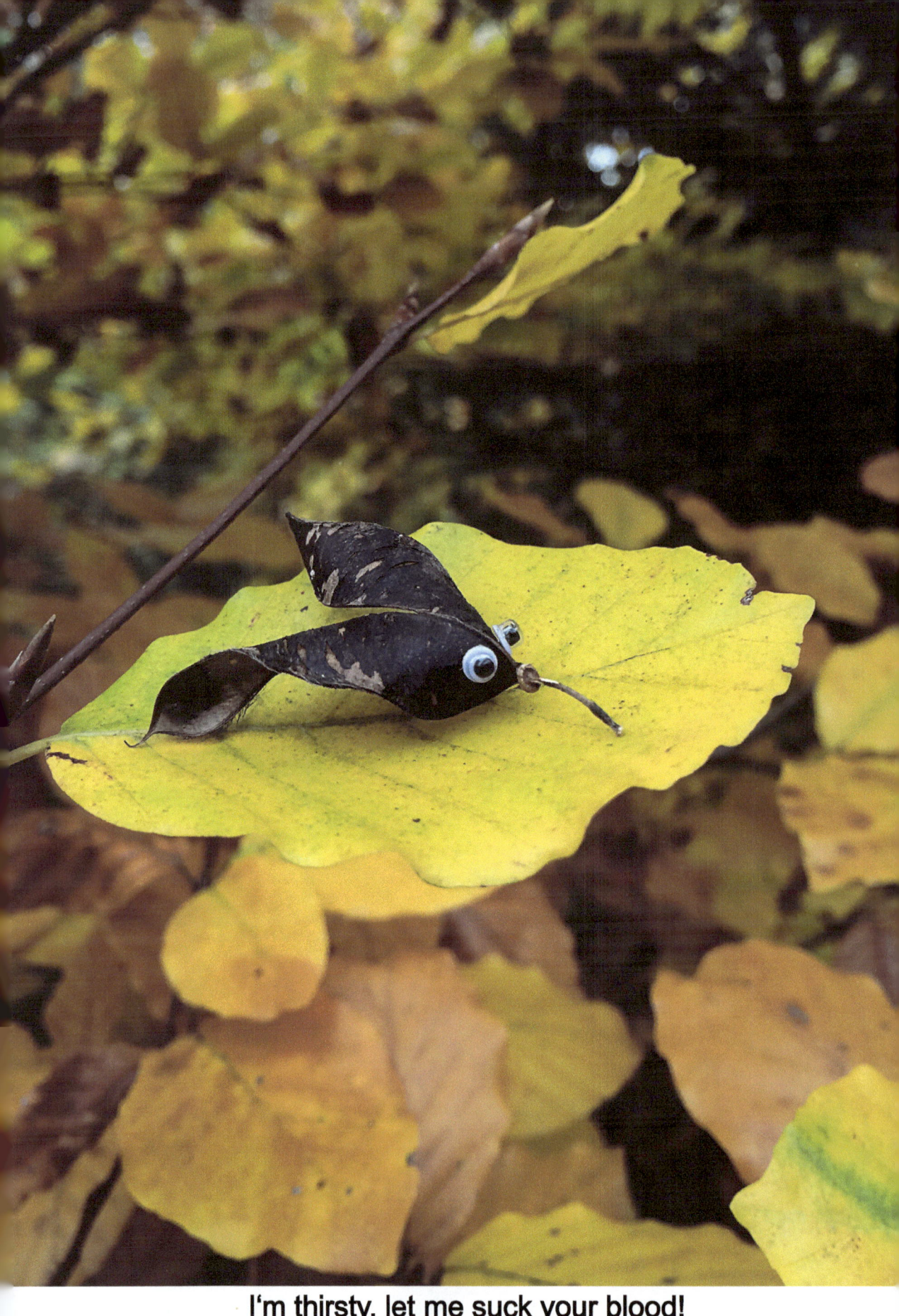

I'm thirsty, let me suck your blood!

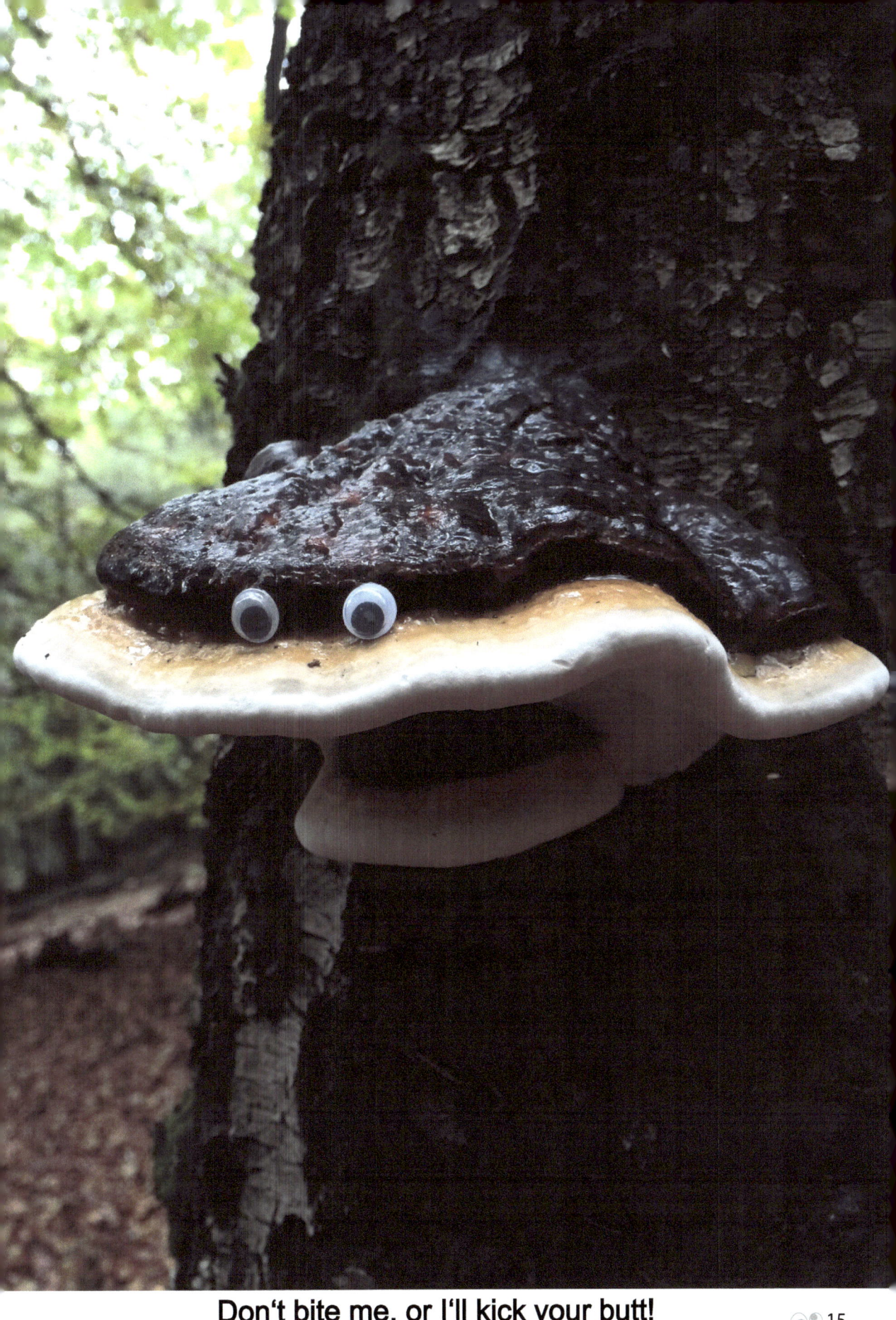

Don't bite me, or I'll kick your butt!

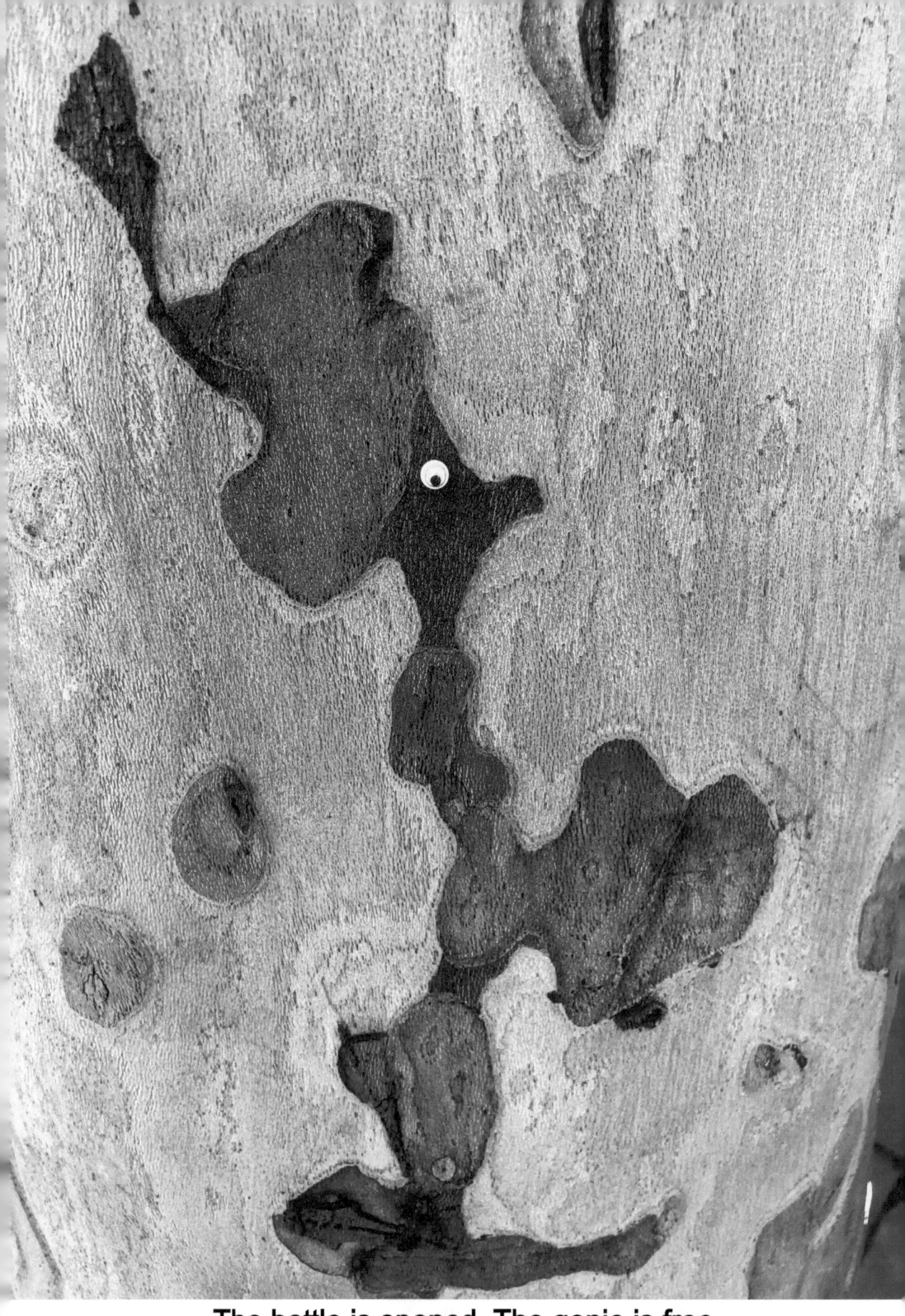

The bottle is opened. The genie is free.

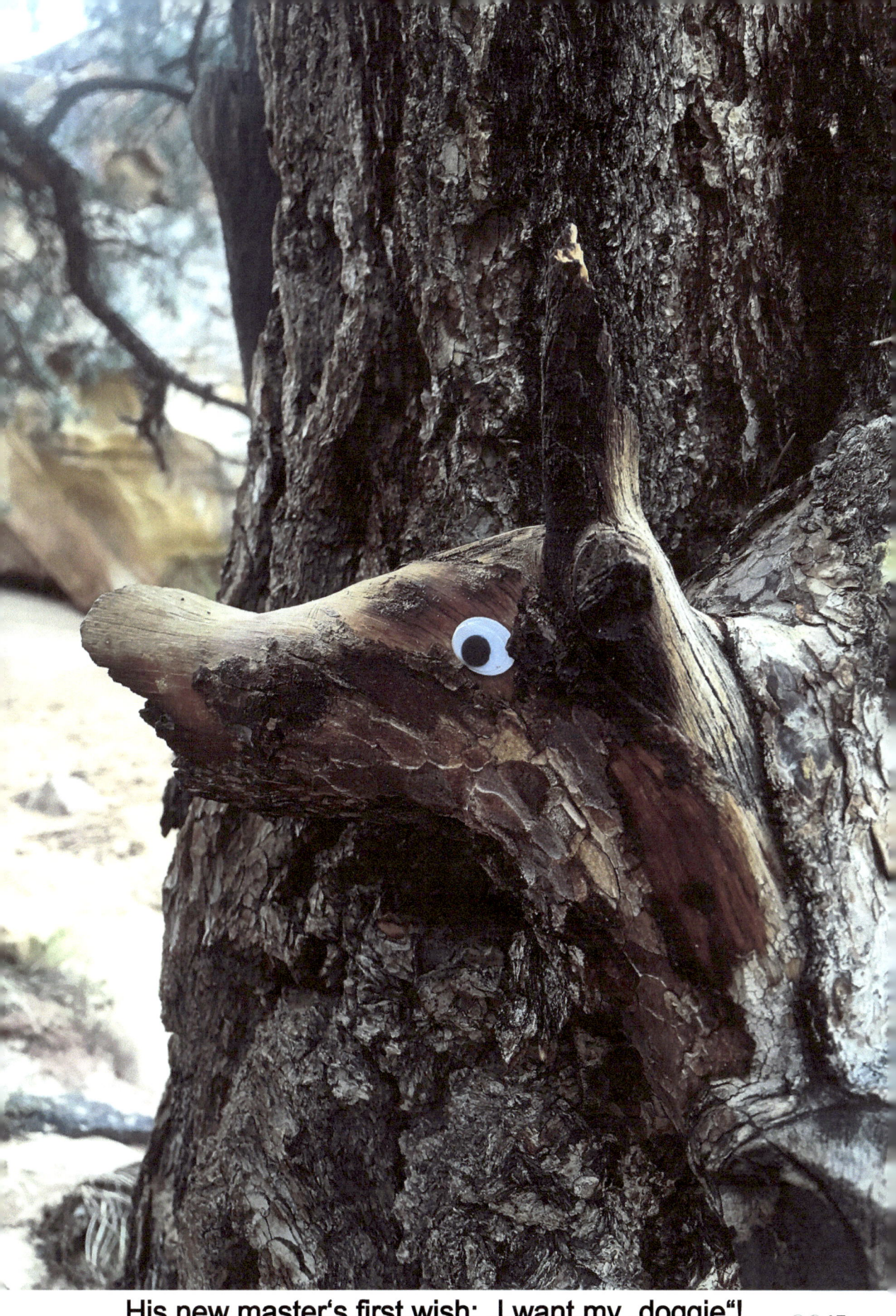

His new master's first wish: „I want my „doggie"!

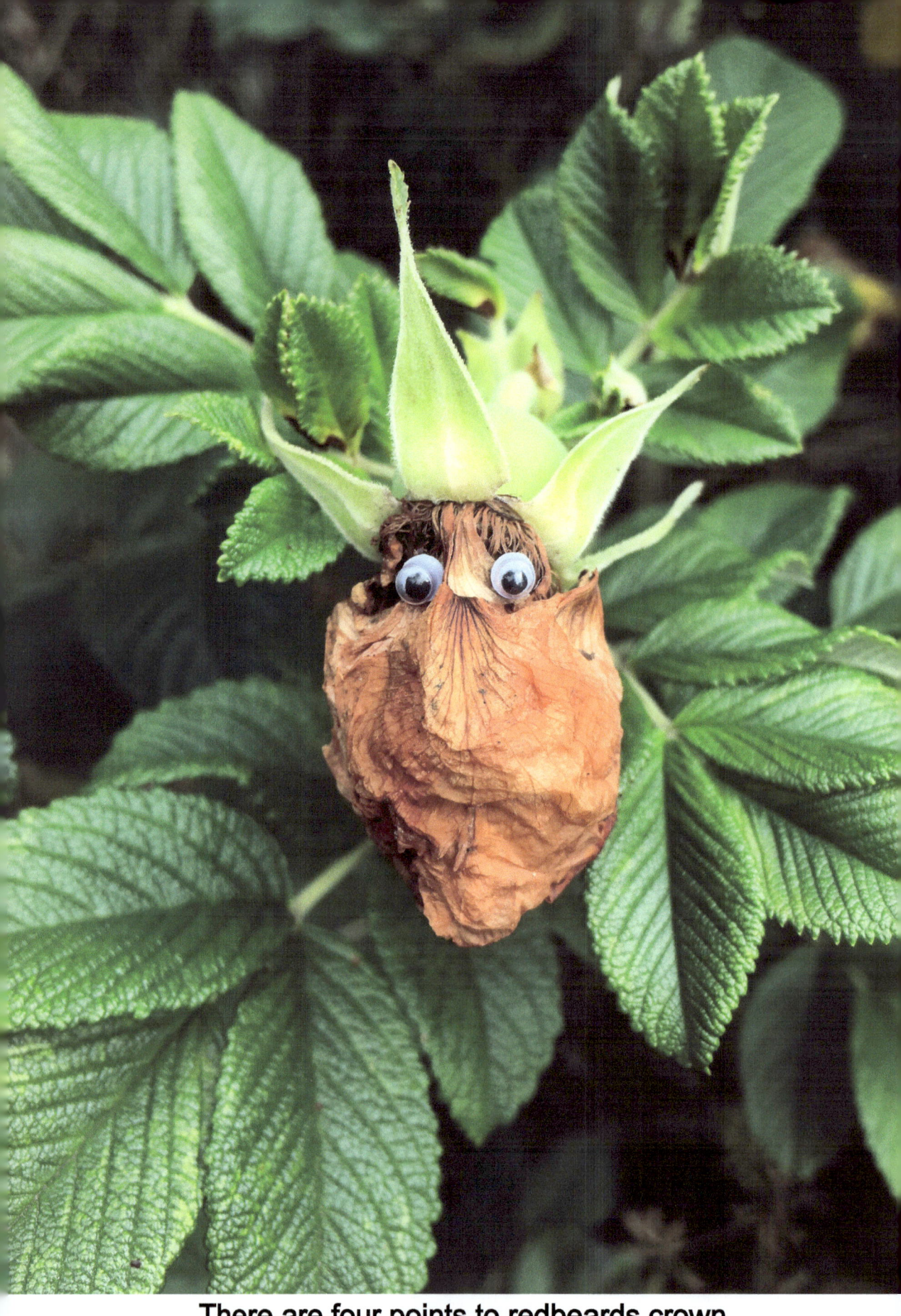
There are four points to redbeards crown.

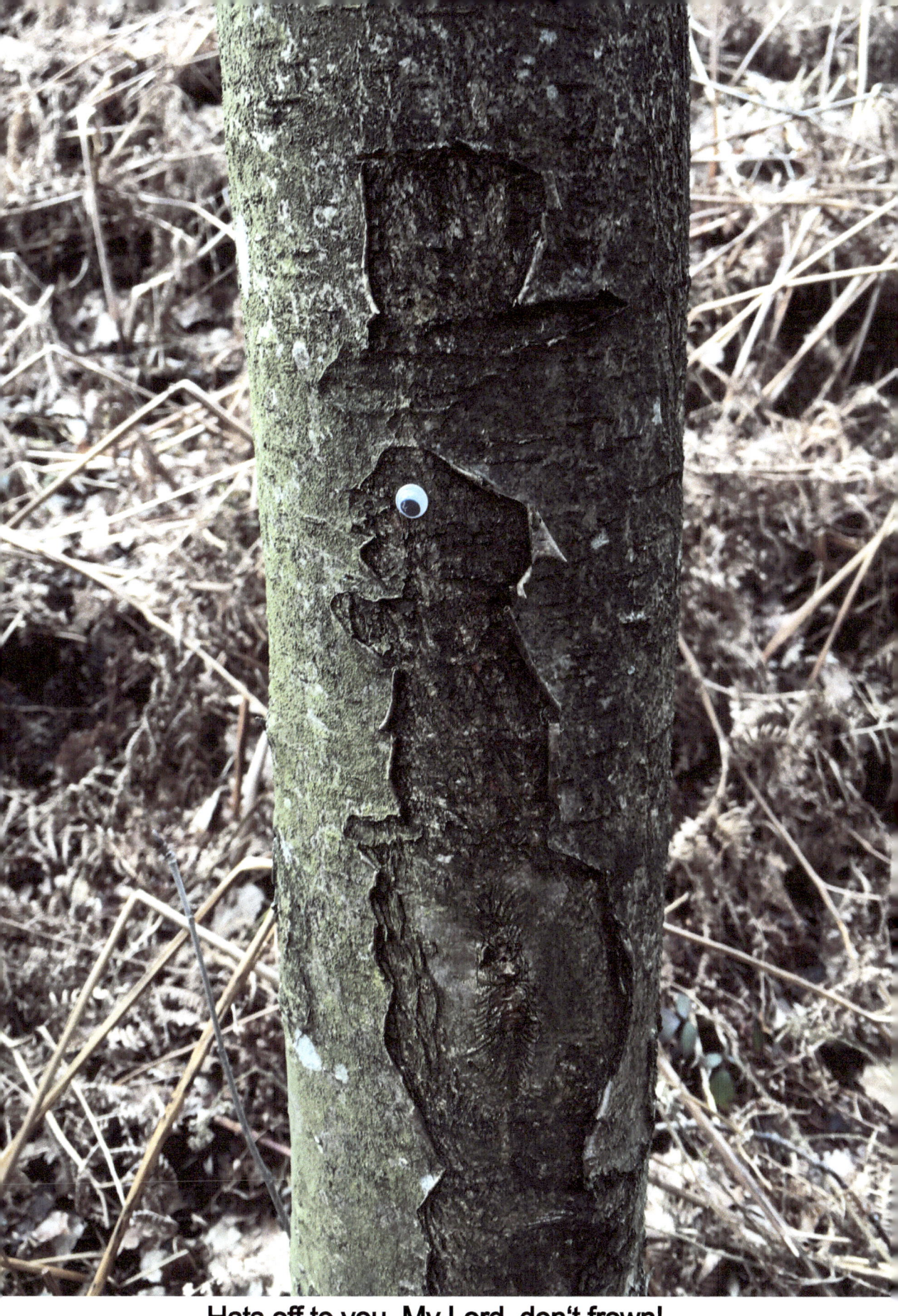
Hats off to you, My Lord, don't frown!

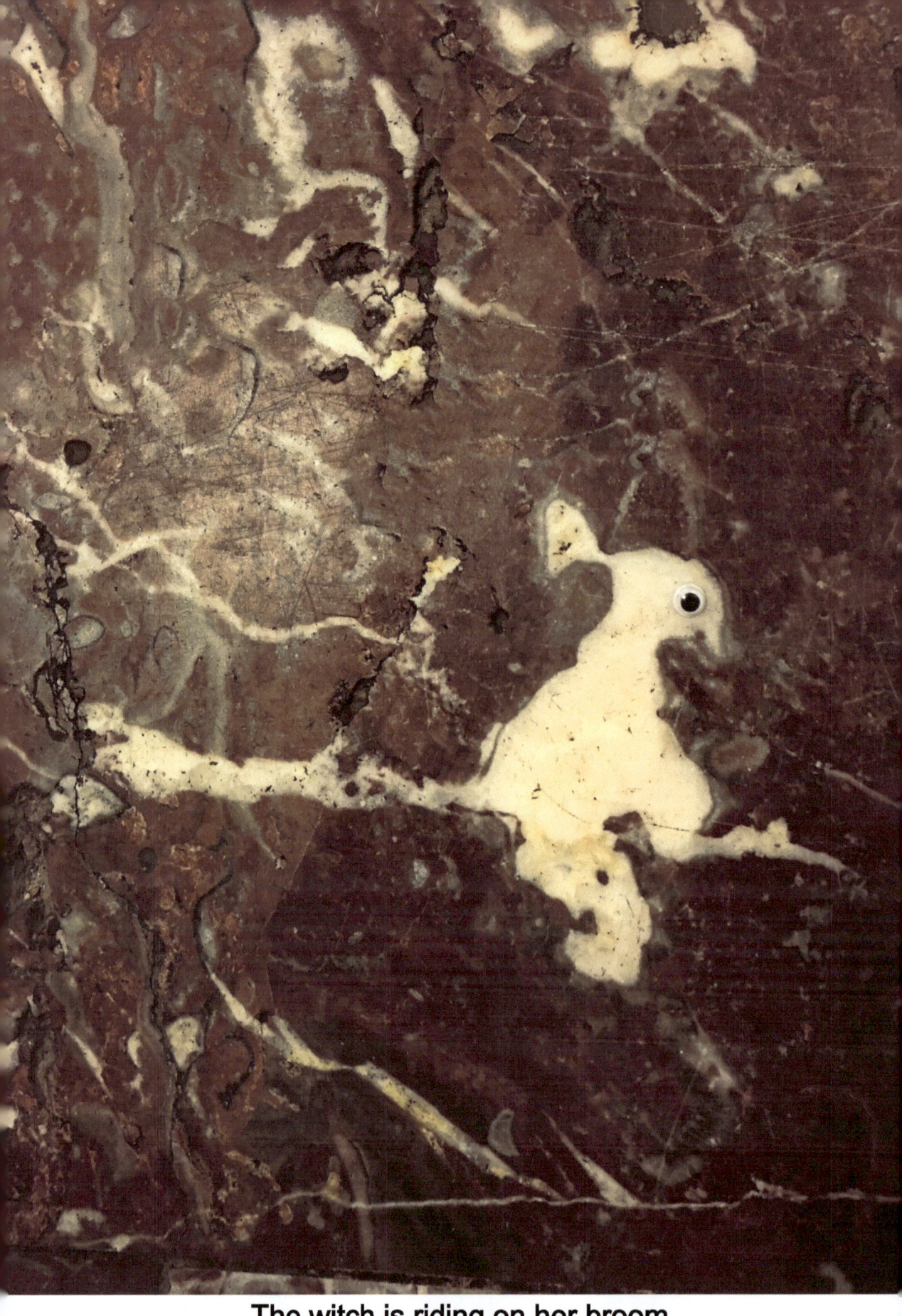

The witch is riding on her broom.

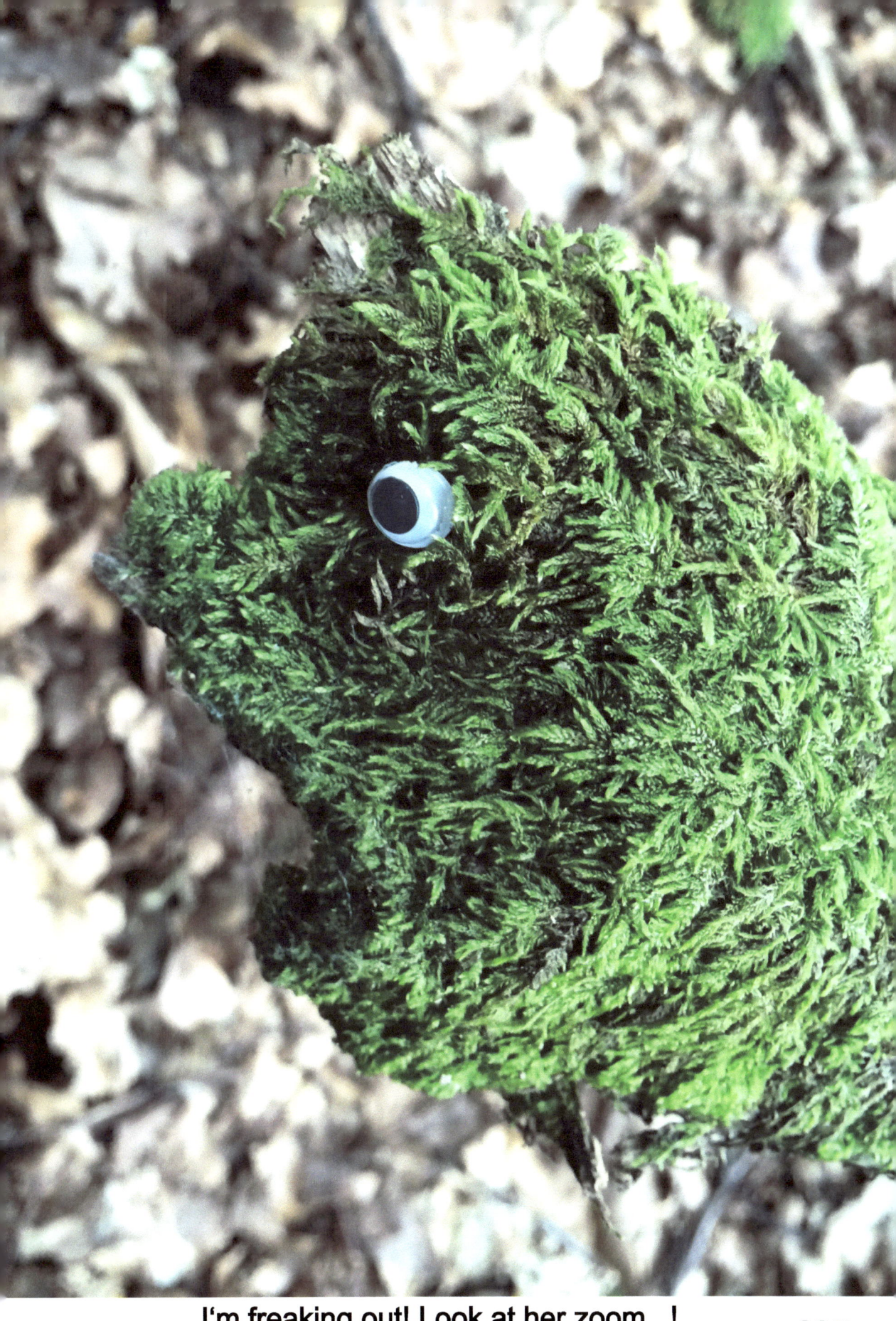
I'm freaking out! Look at her zoom...!

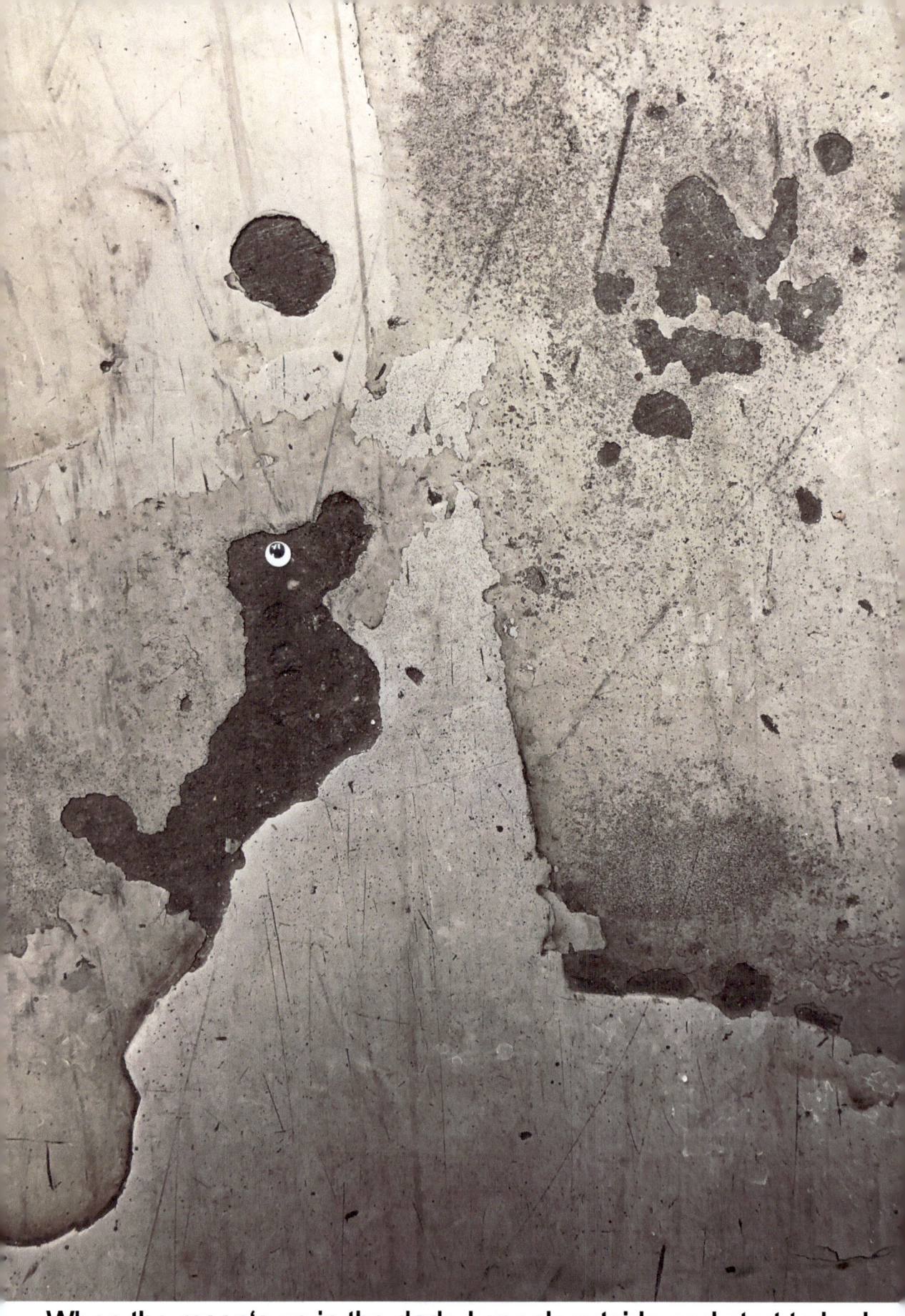

When the moon's up in the dark, I sneak outside and start to bark.

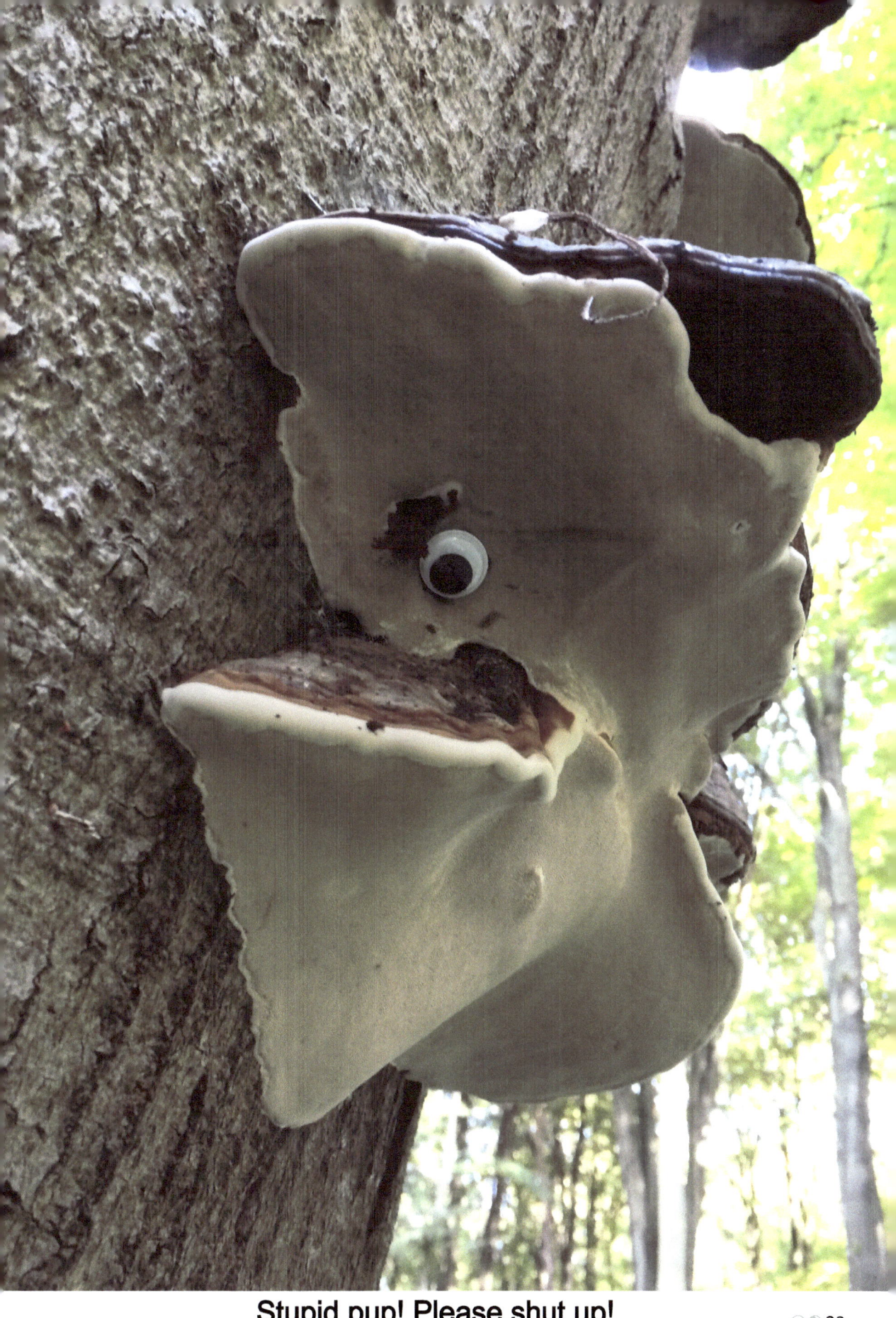

Stupid pup! Please shut up!

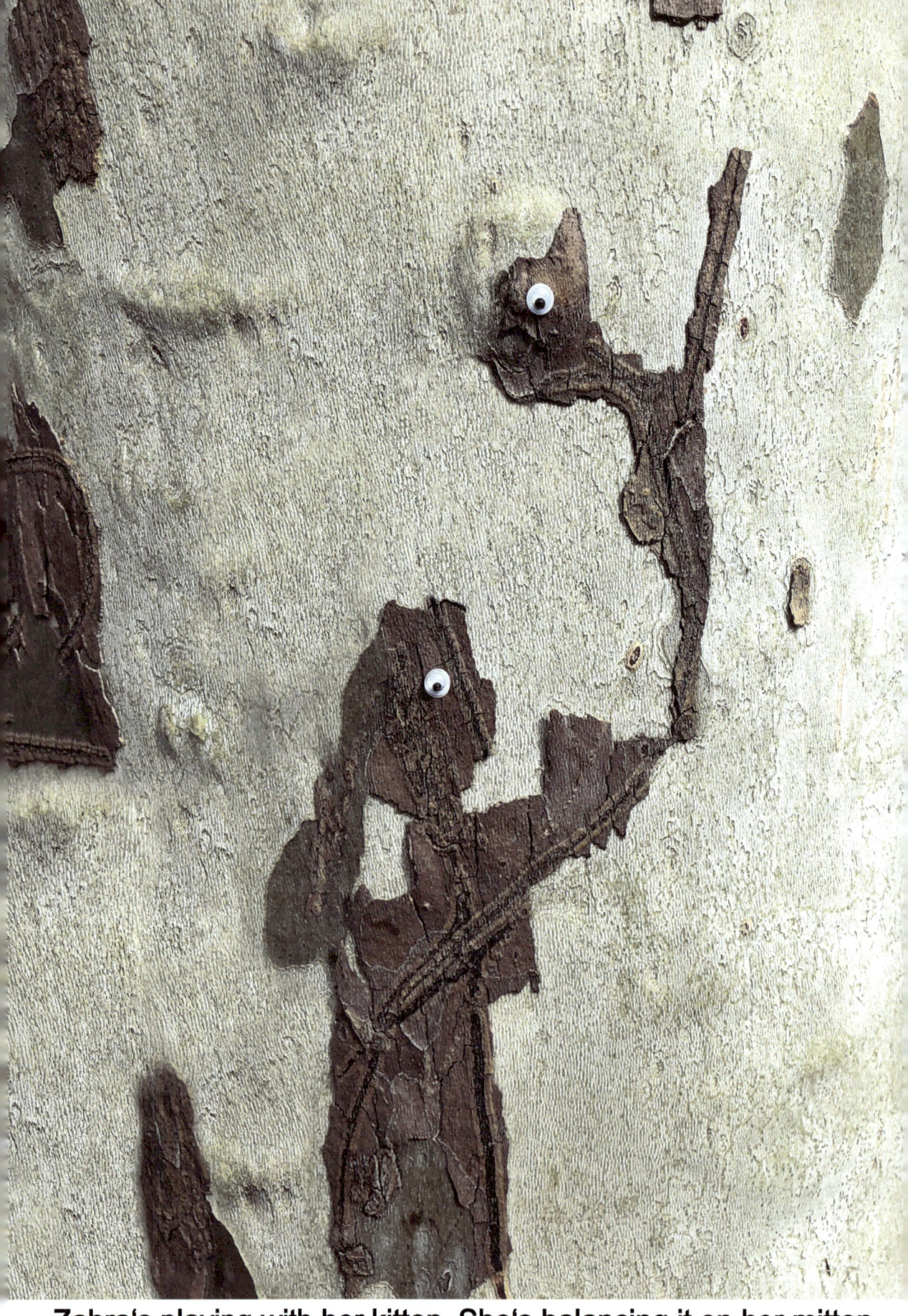
Zahra's playing with her kitten. She's balancing it on her mitten.

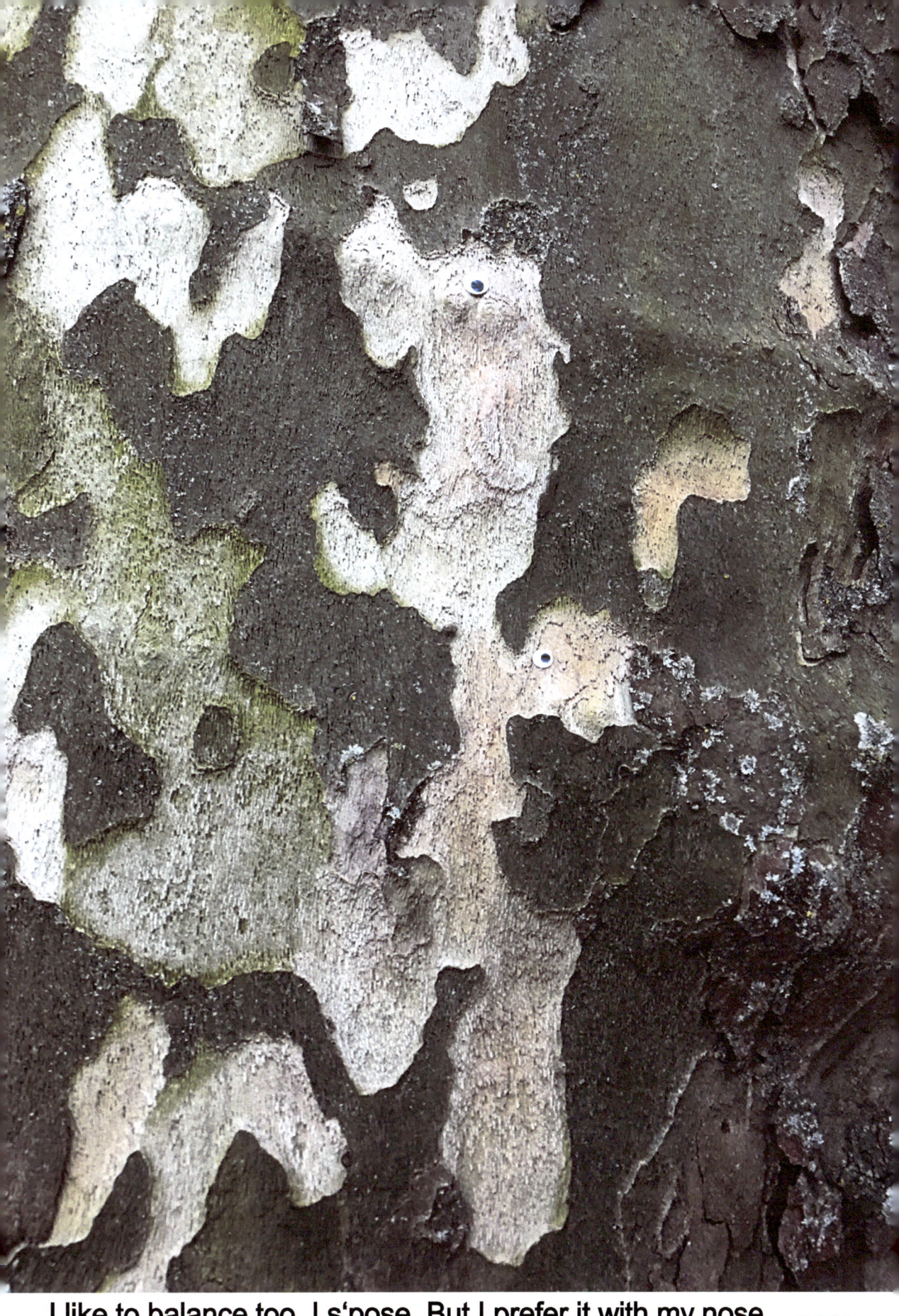
I like to balance too, I s'pose. But I prefer it with my nose.

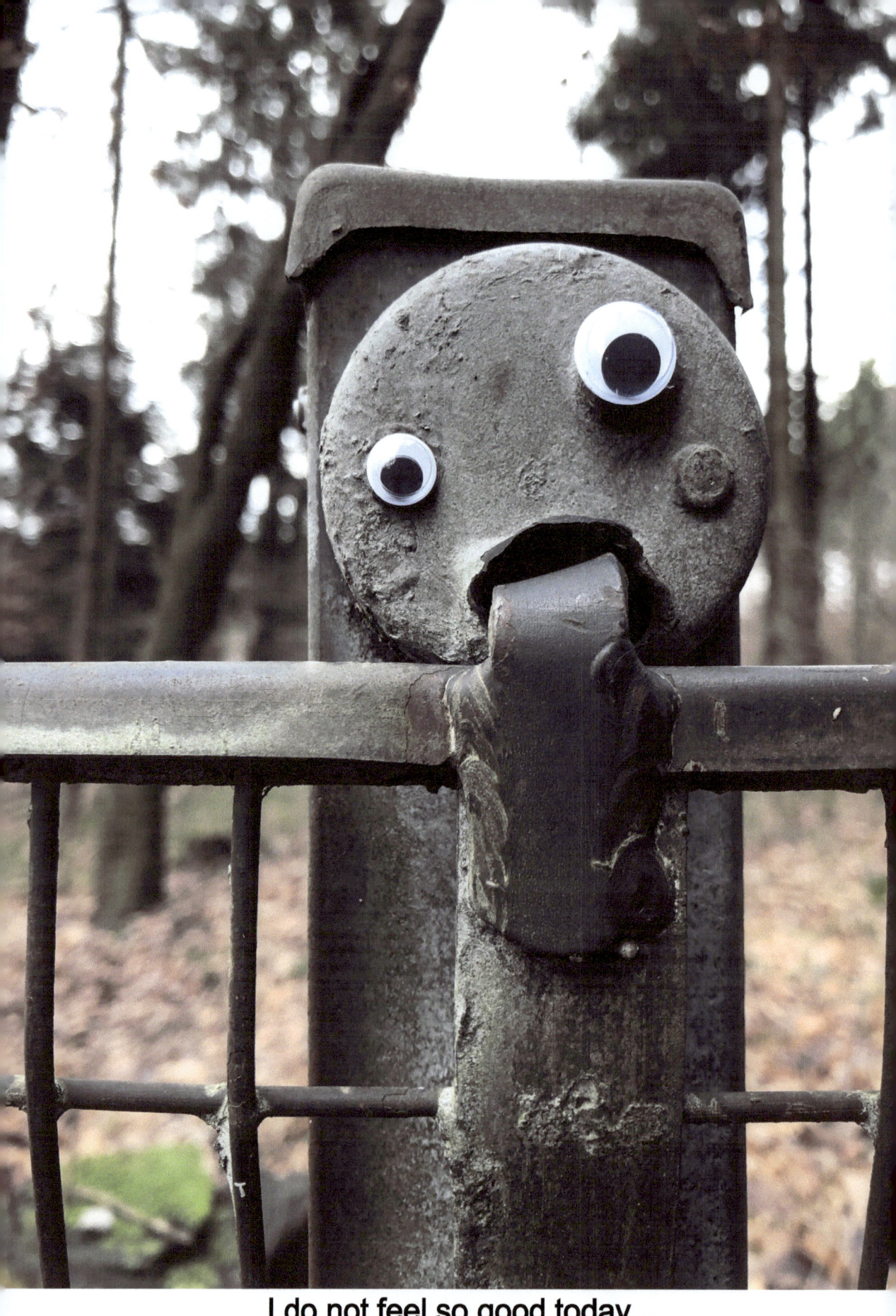
I do not feel so good today...

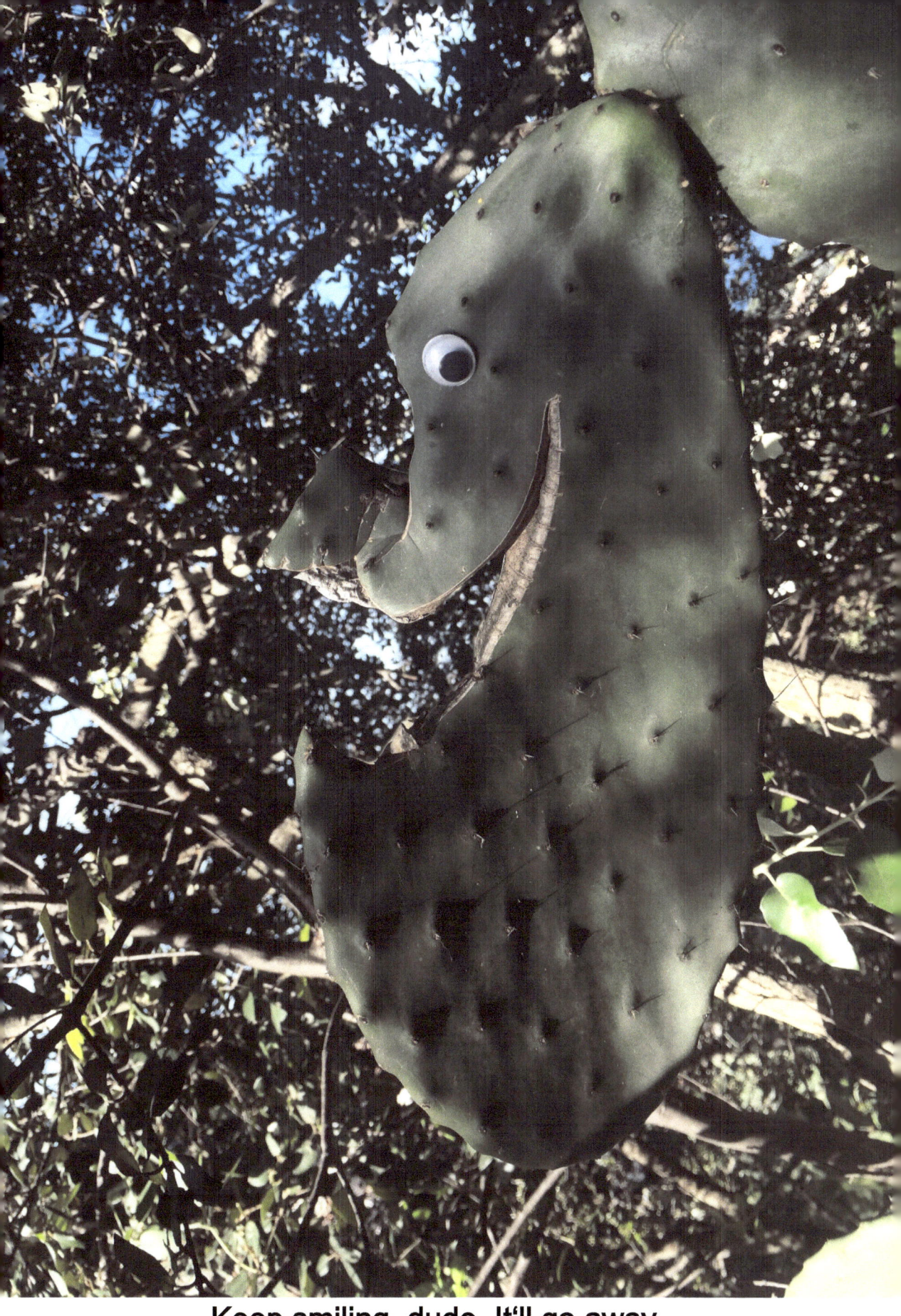

Keep smiling, dude. It'll go away.

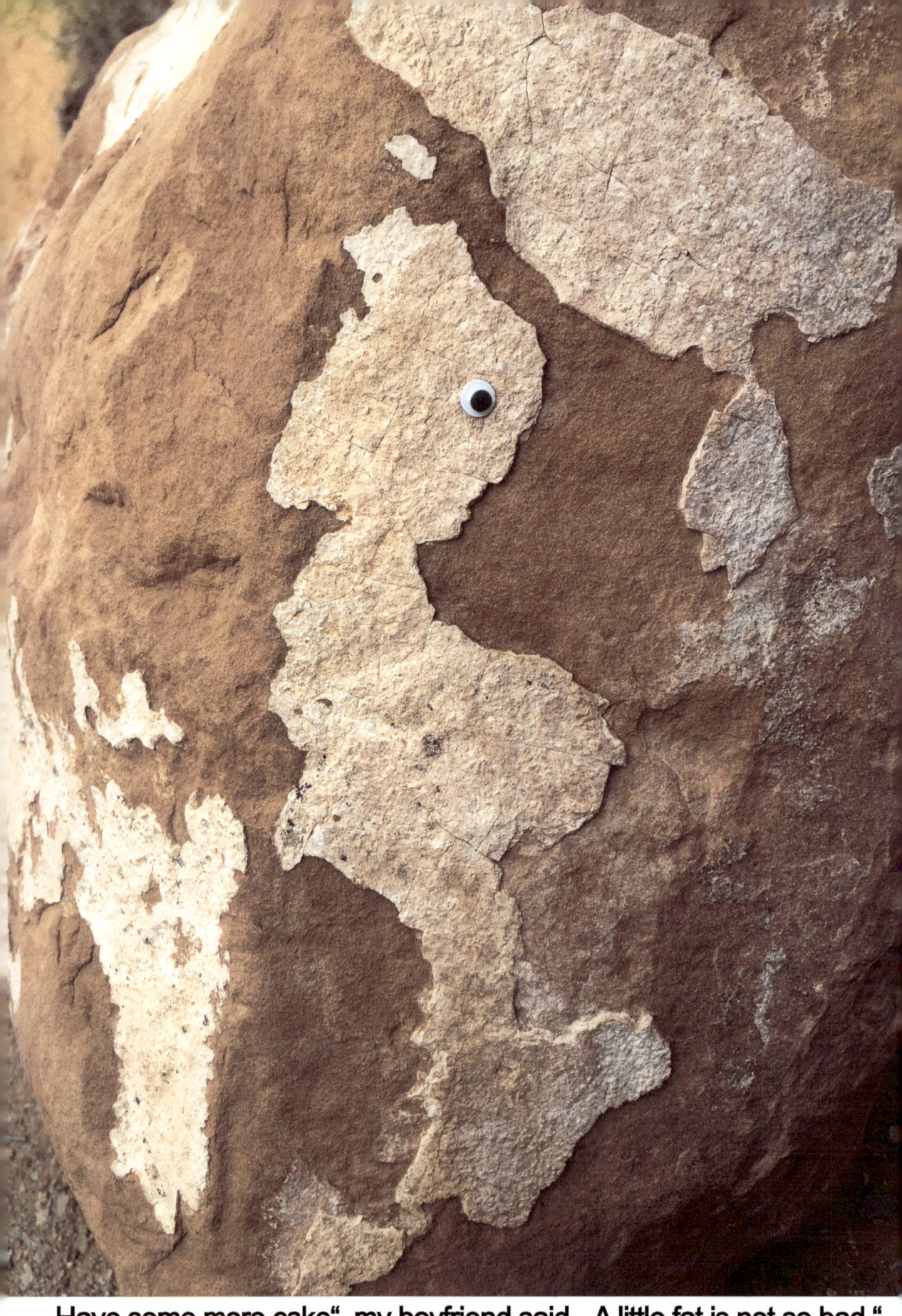

„Have some more cake", my boyfriend said. „A little fat is not so bad."

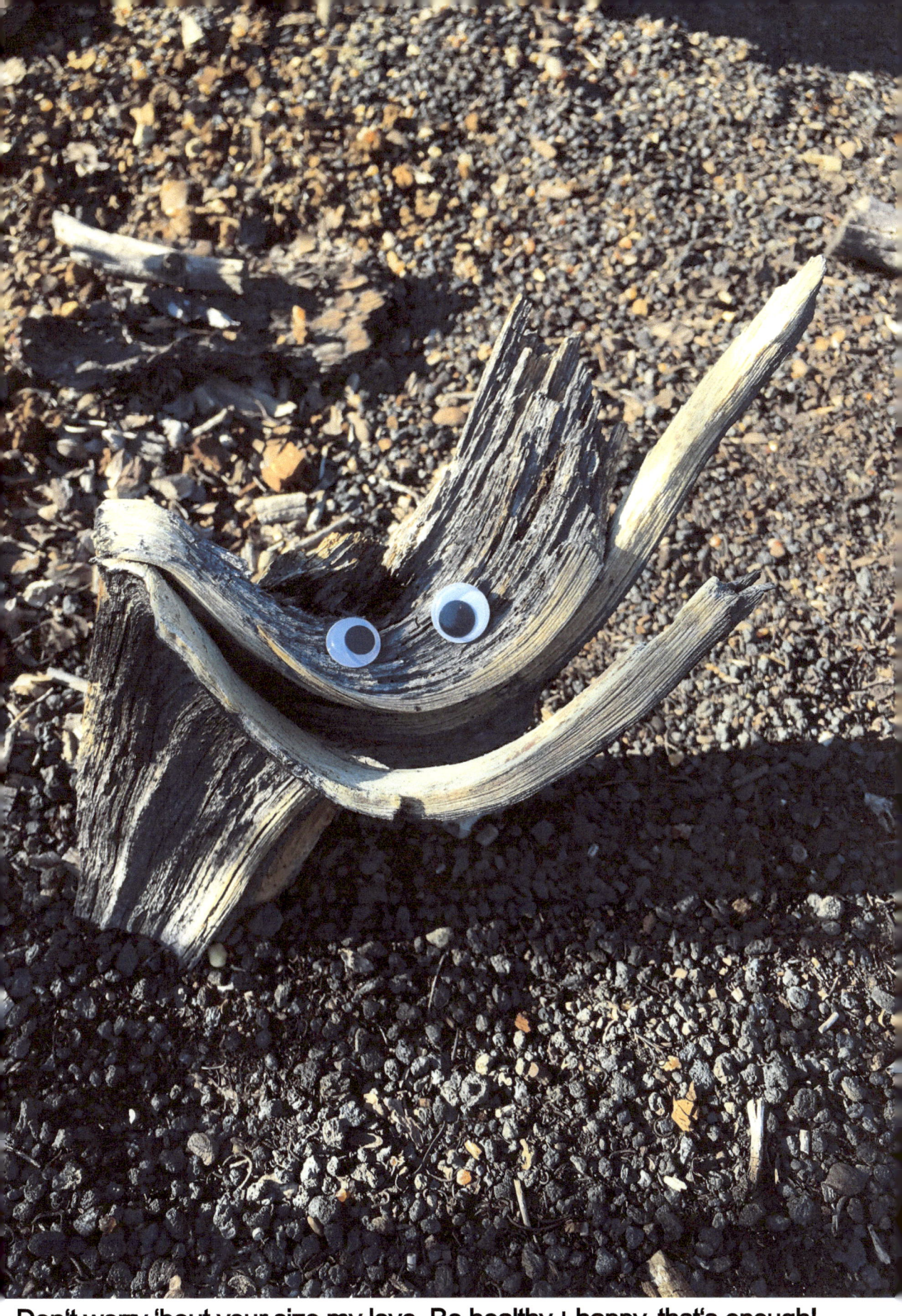
Don't worry 'bout your size my love. Be healthy + happy, that's enough!

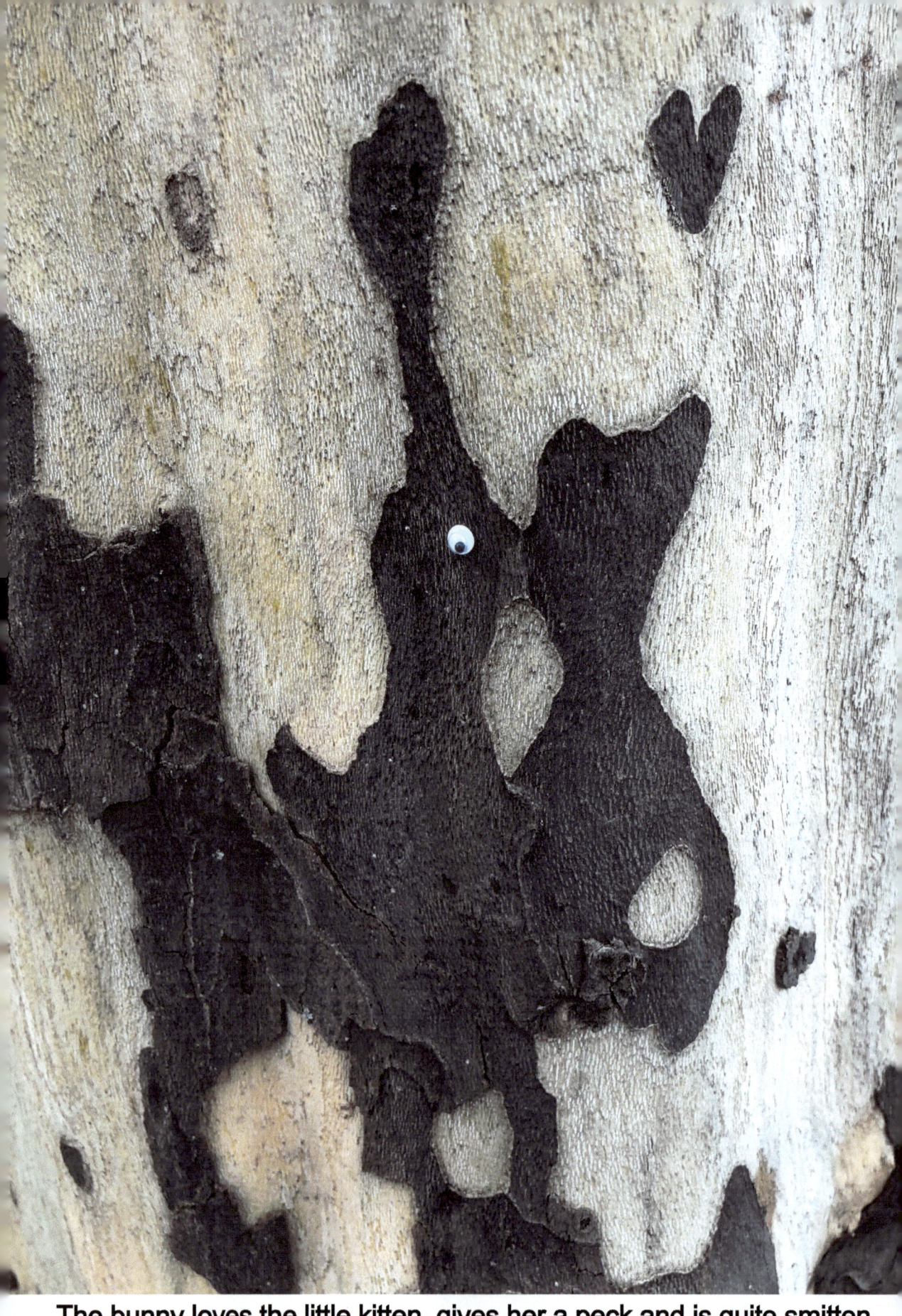
The bunny loves the little kitten, gives her a peck and is quite smitten.

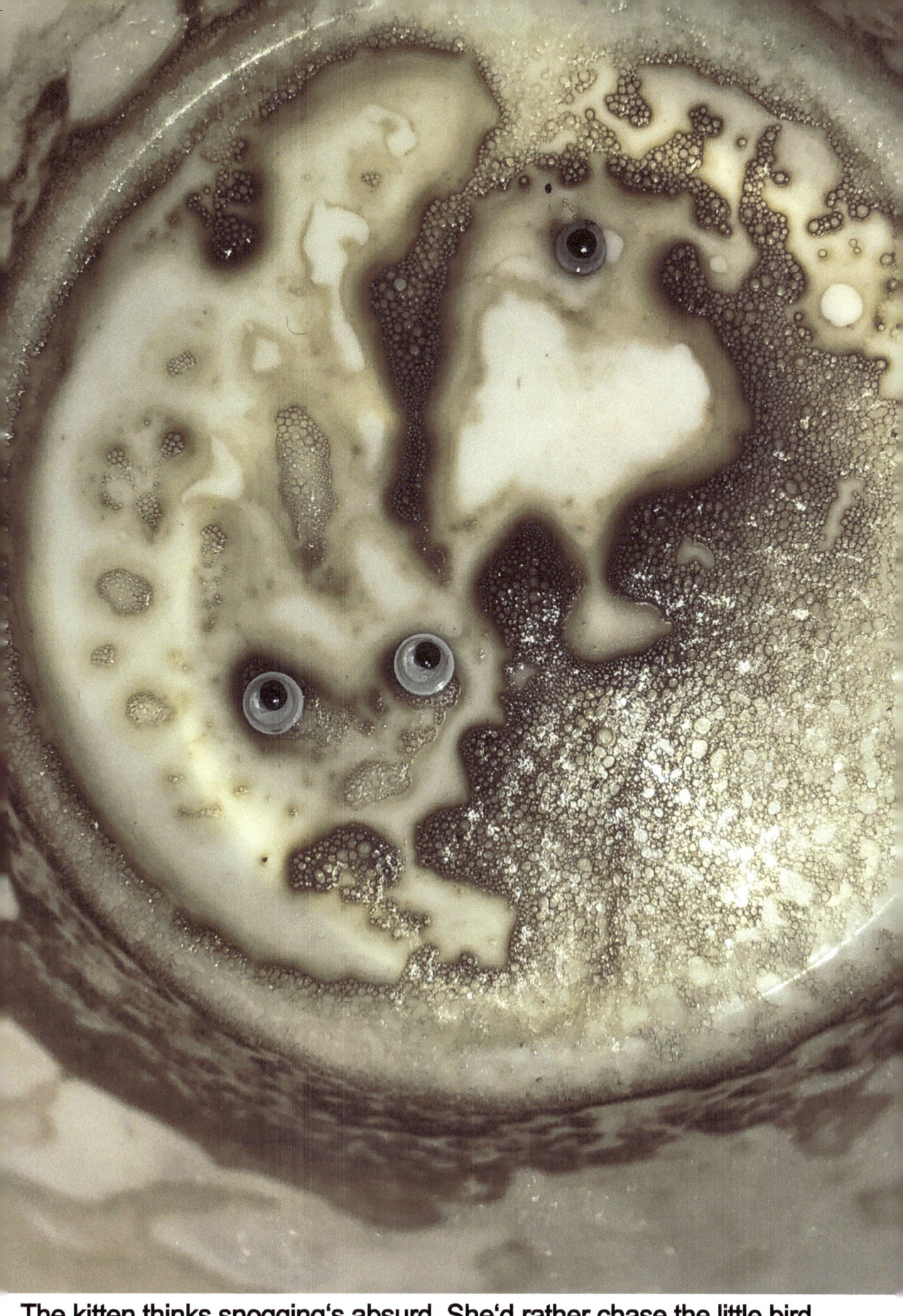
The kitten thinks snogging's absurd. She'd rather chase the little bird.

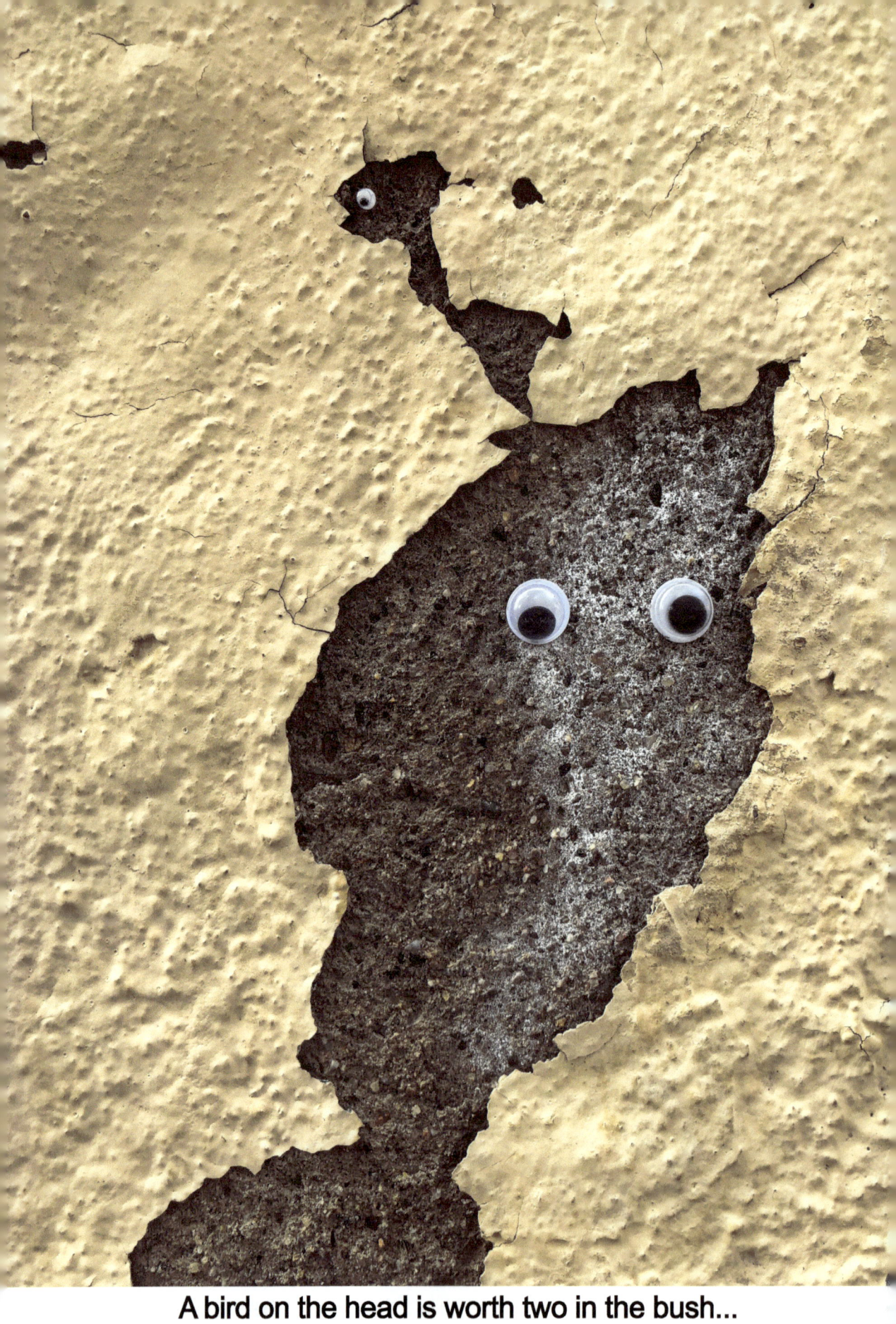

A bird on the head is worth two in the bush...

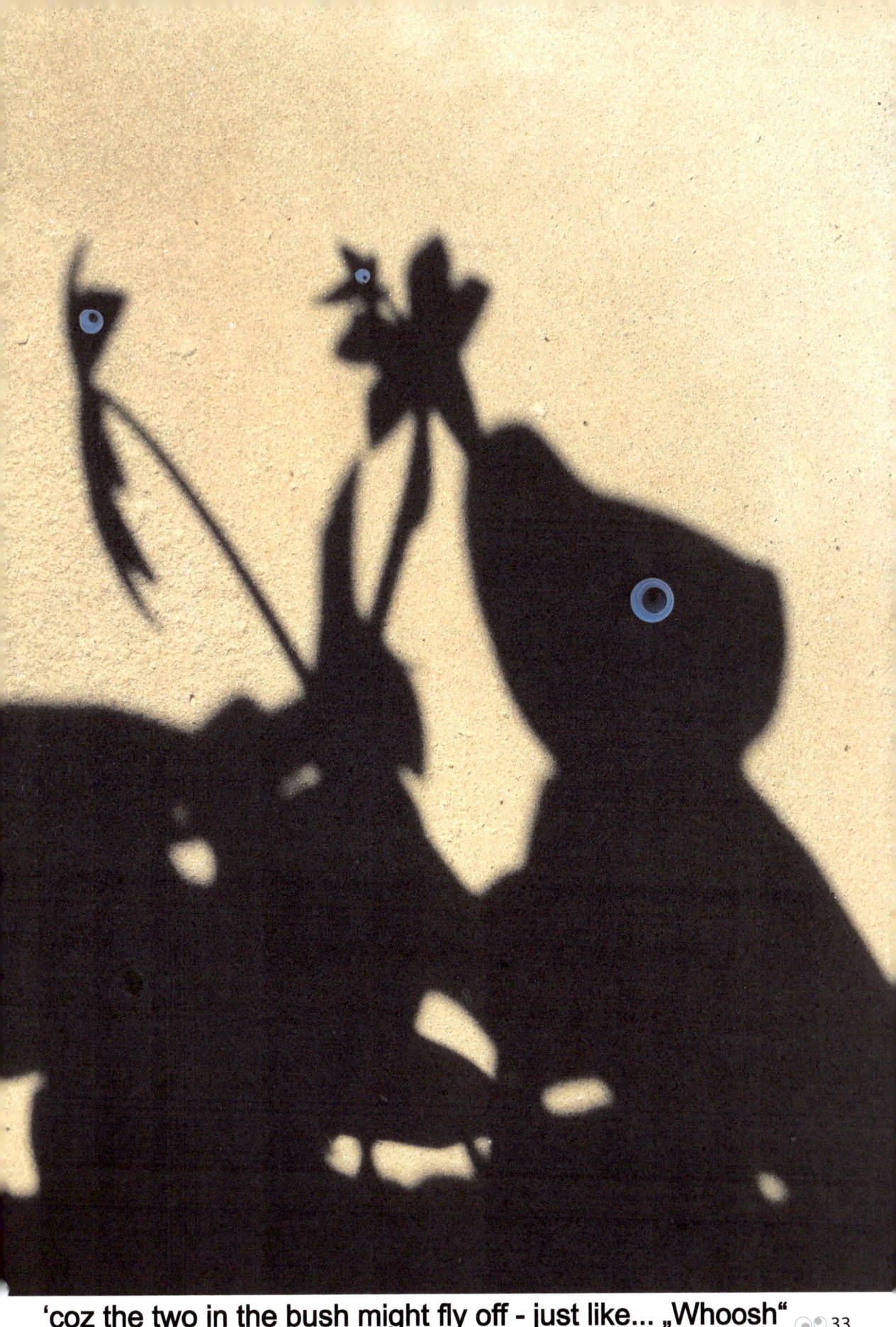
'coz the two in the bush might fly off - just like... „Whoosh"

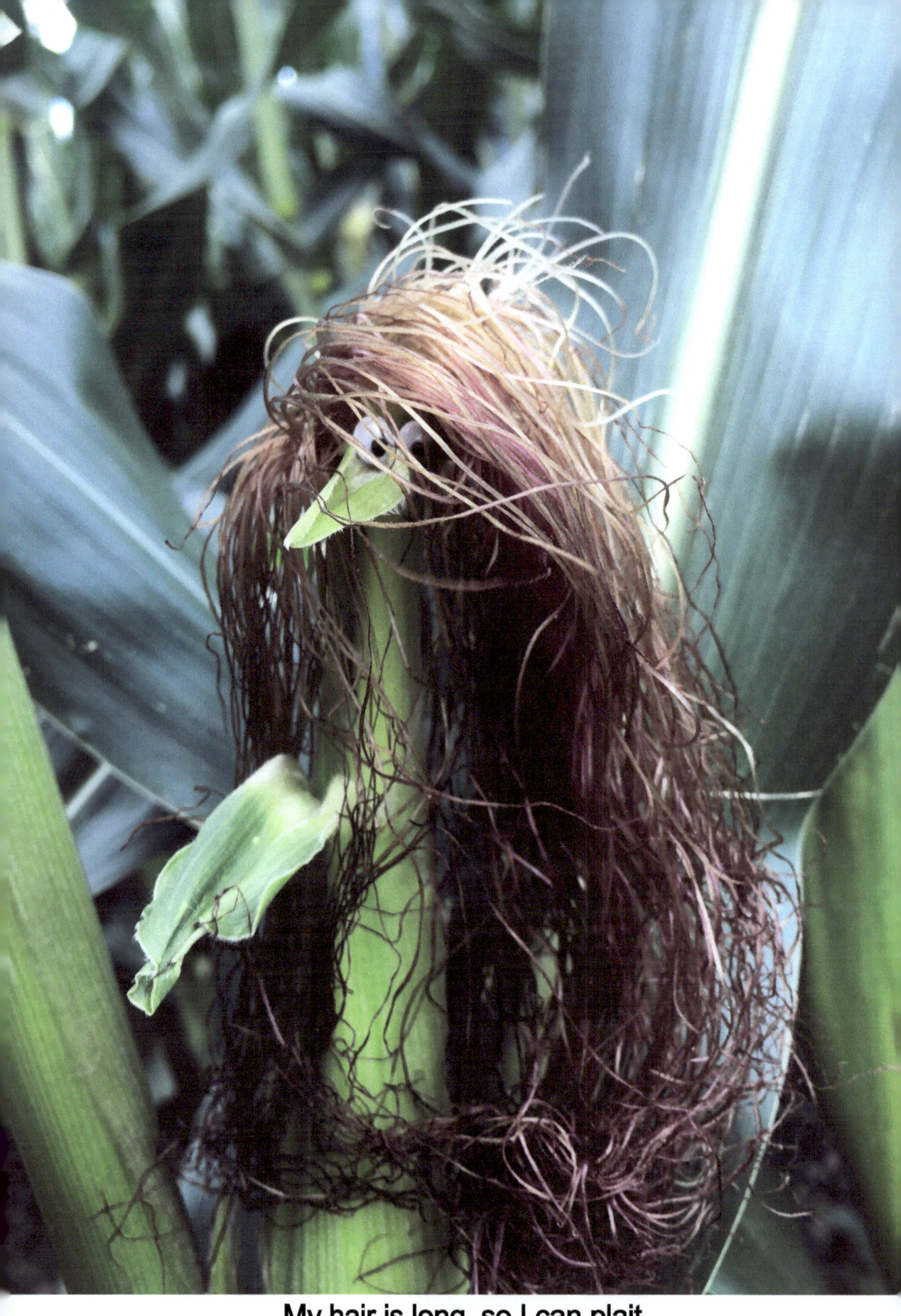

My hair is long, so I can plait.

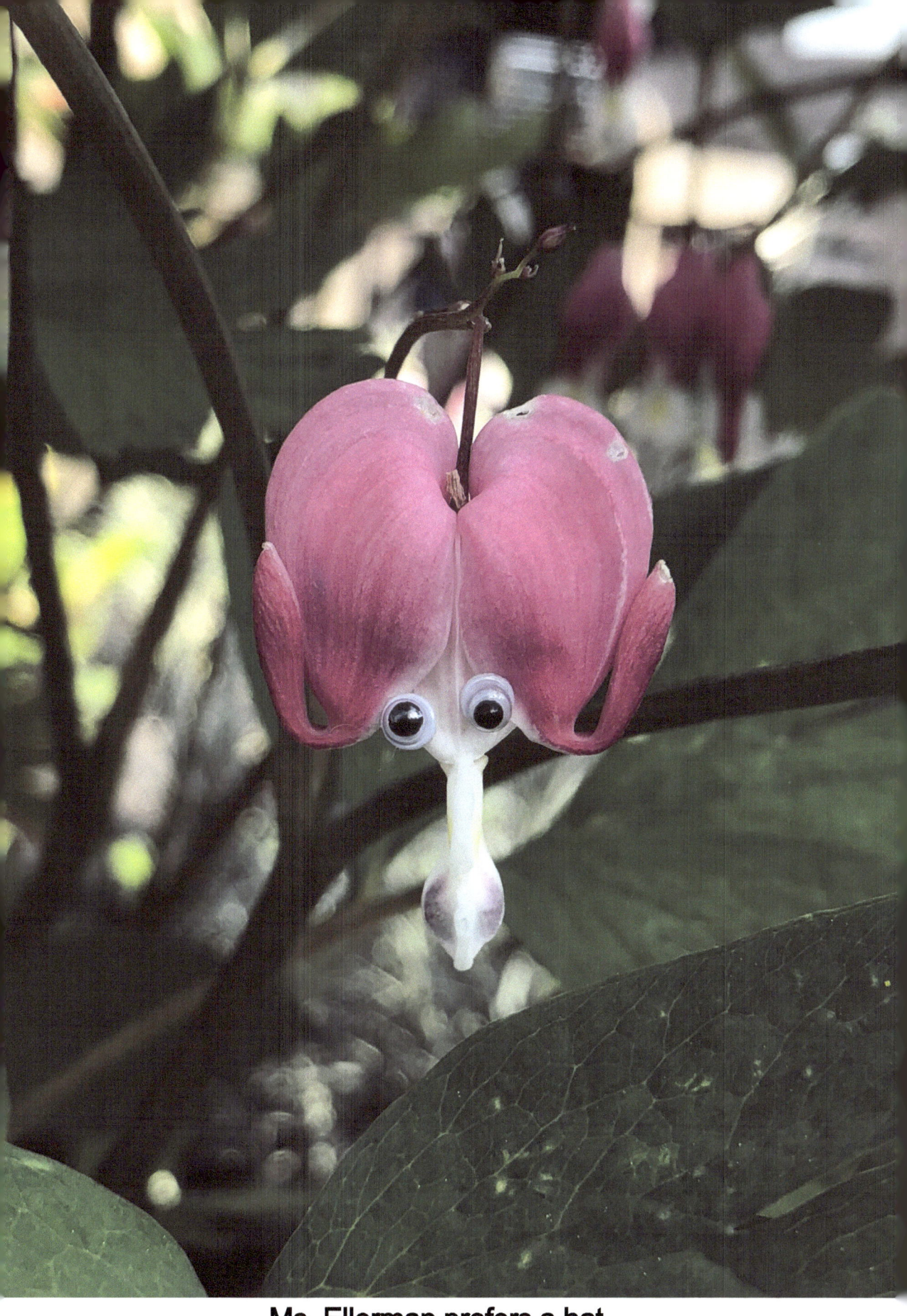

Ms. Ellerman prefers a hat.

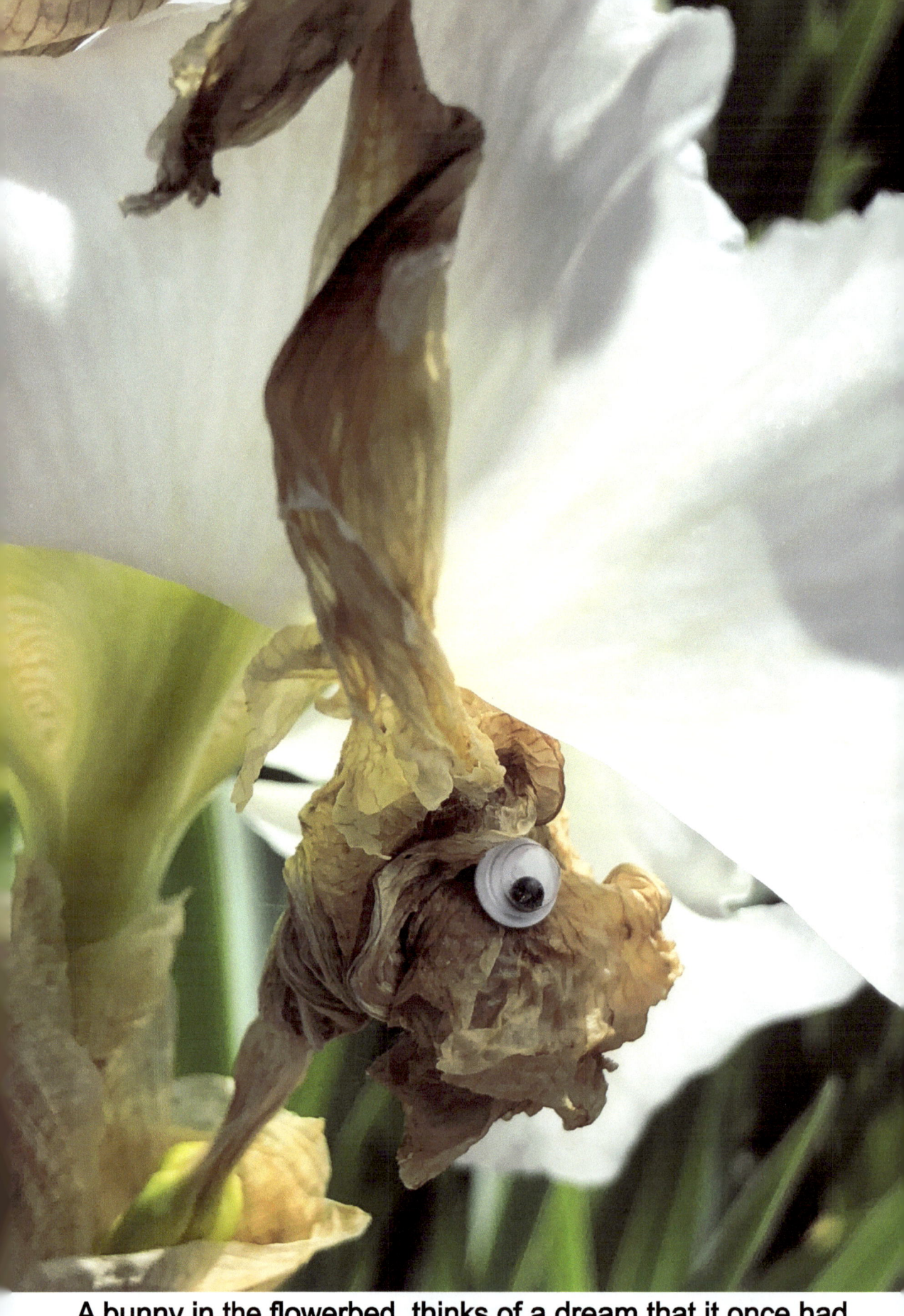

A bunny in the flowerbed, thinks of a dream that it once had.

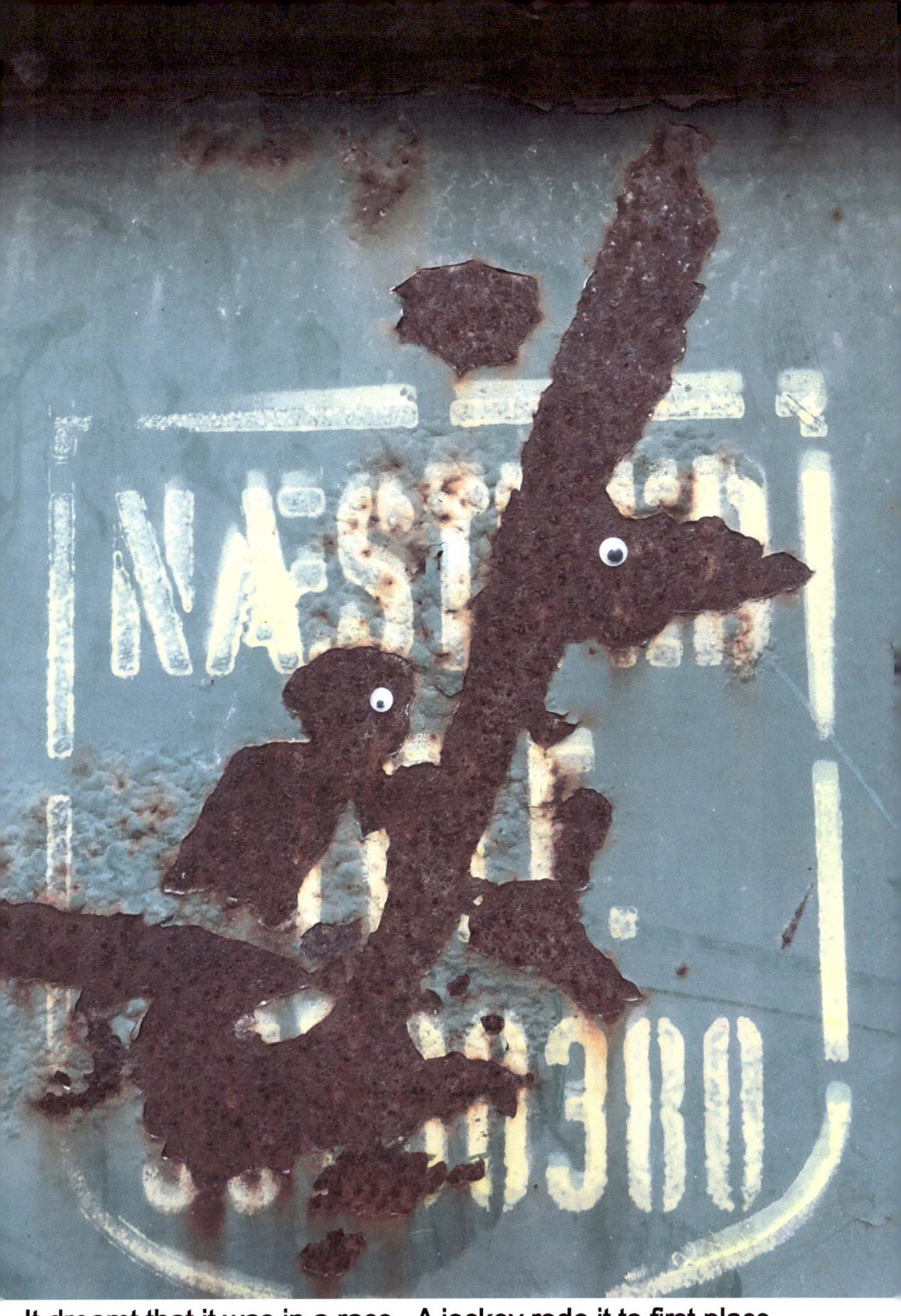
It dreamt that it was in a race. A jockey rode it to first place.

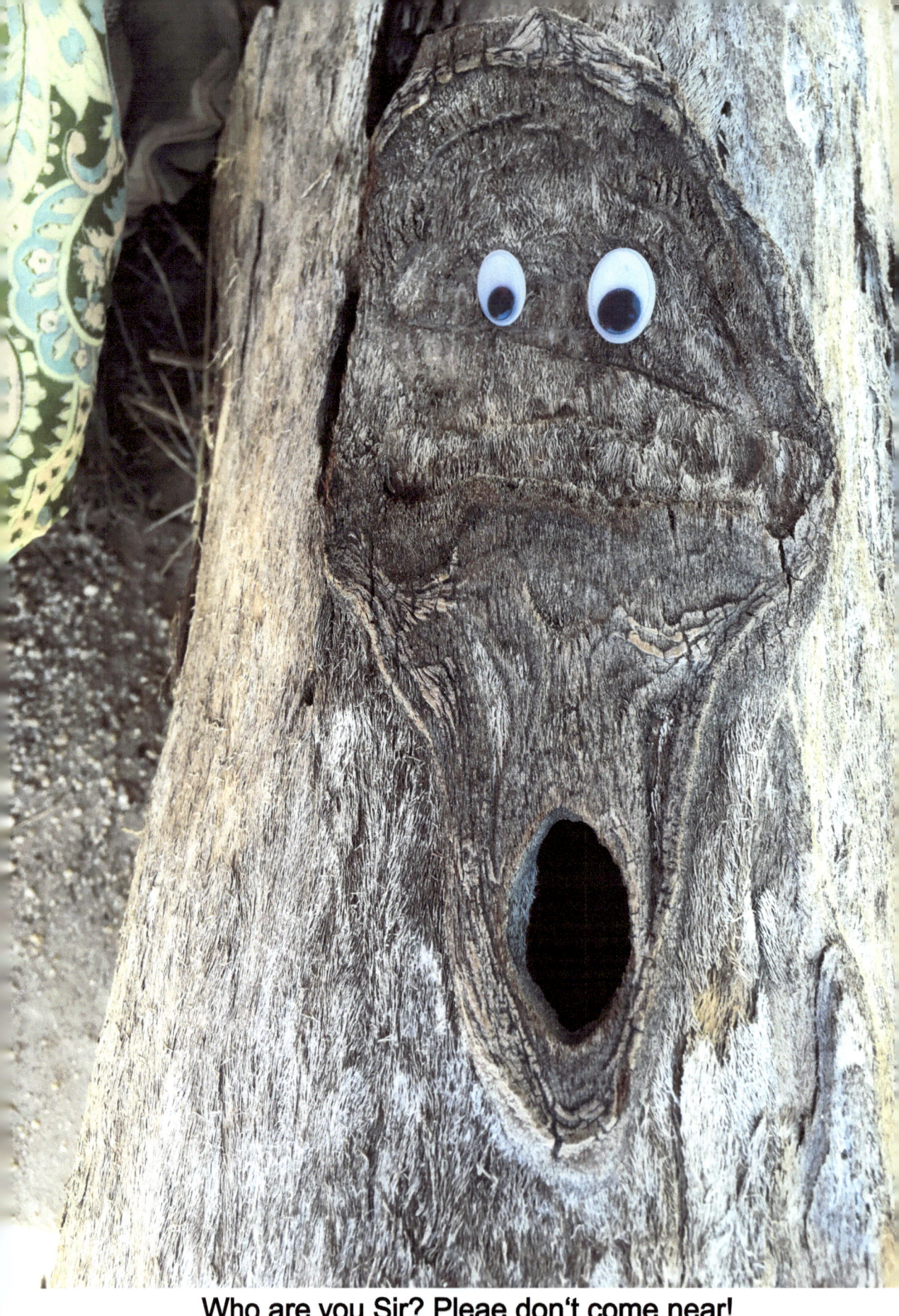

Who are you Sir? Pleae don't come near!

I'm Dracula. No need to fear.

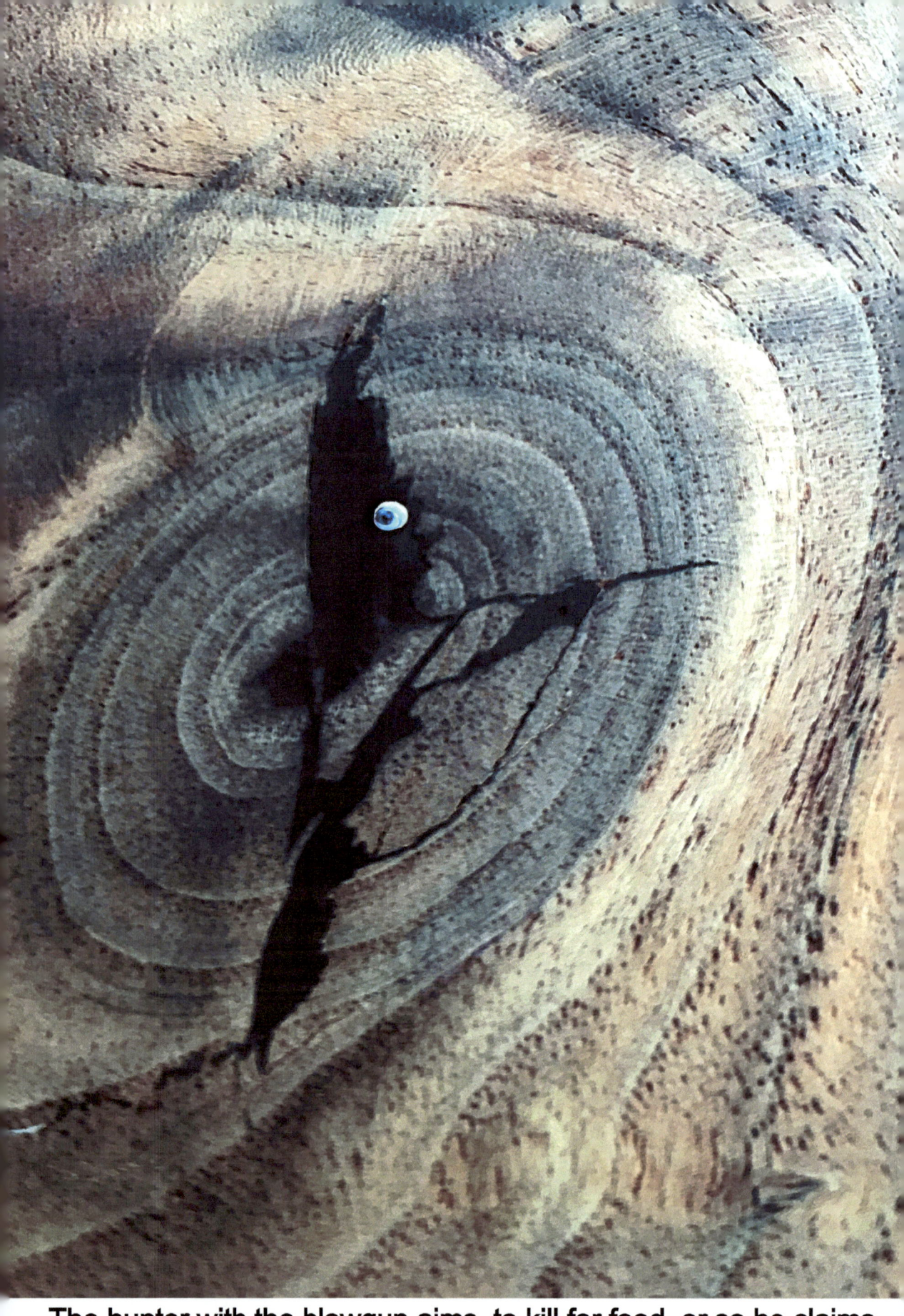

The hunter with the blowgun aims, to kill for food, or so he claims.

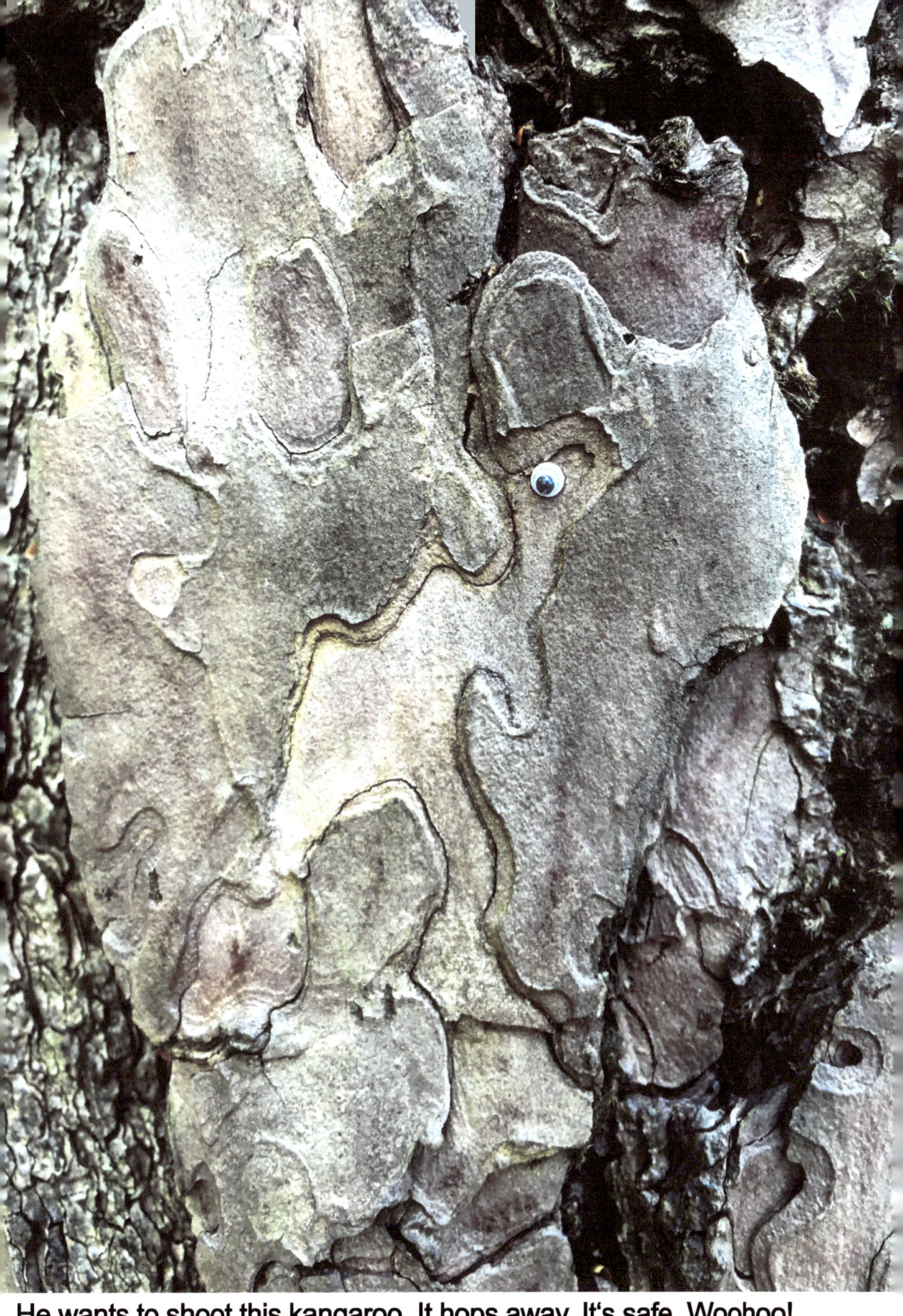
He wants to shoot this kangaroo. It hops away. It's safe. Woohoo!

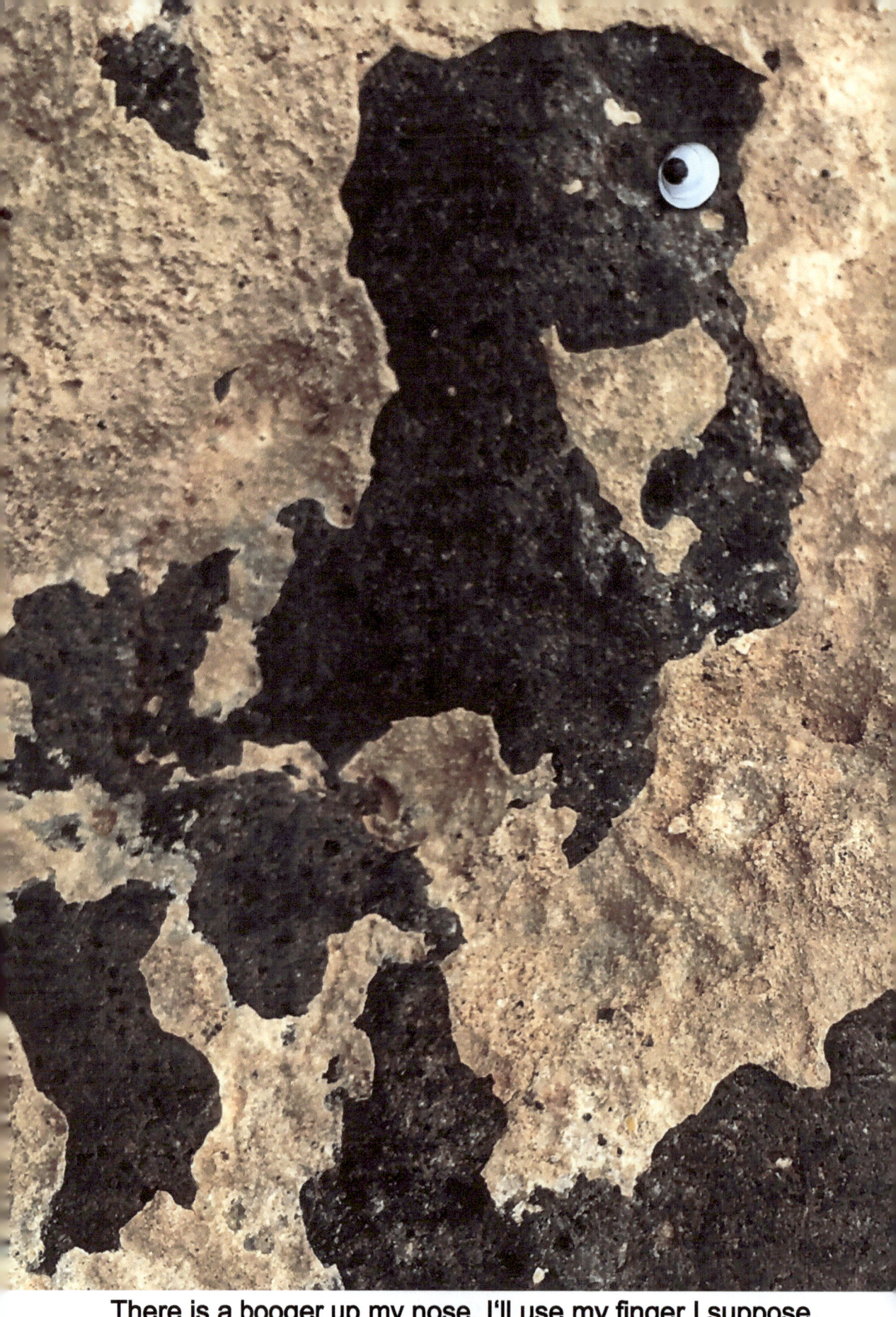
There is a booger up my nose. I'll use my finger I suppose.

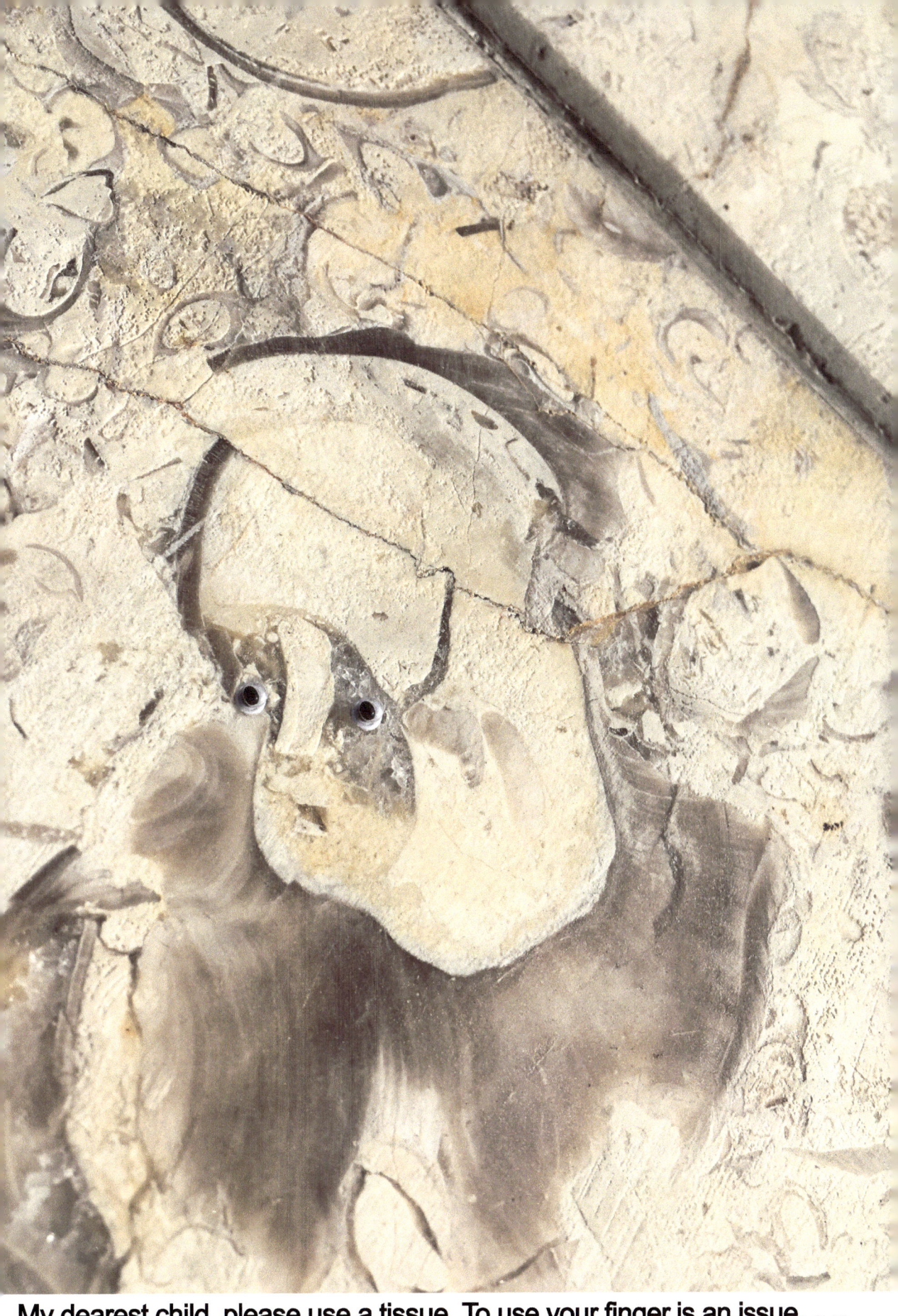

My dearest child, please use a tissue. To use your finger is an issue.

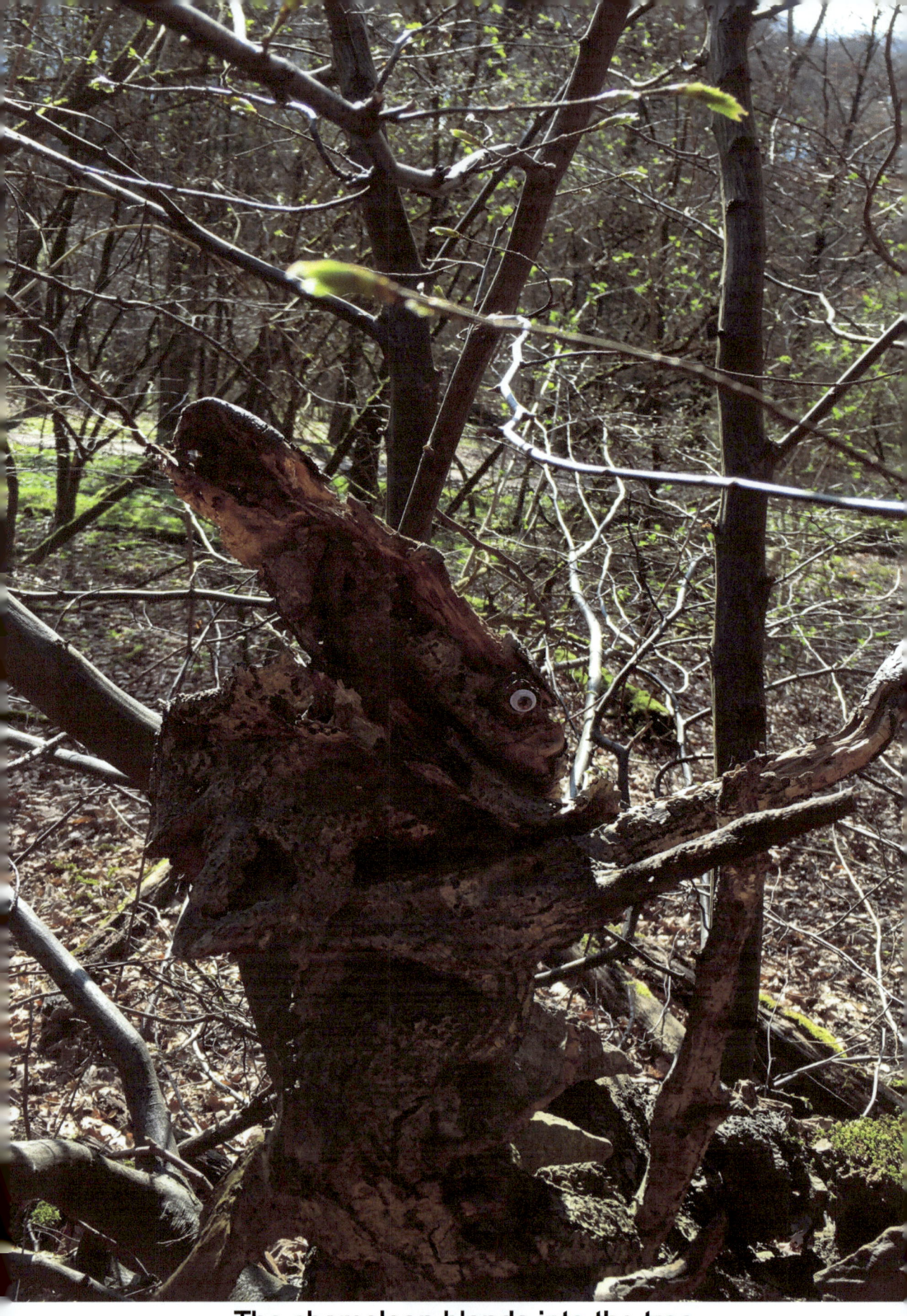
The chameleon blends into the tree.

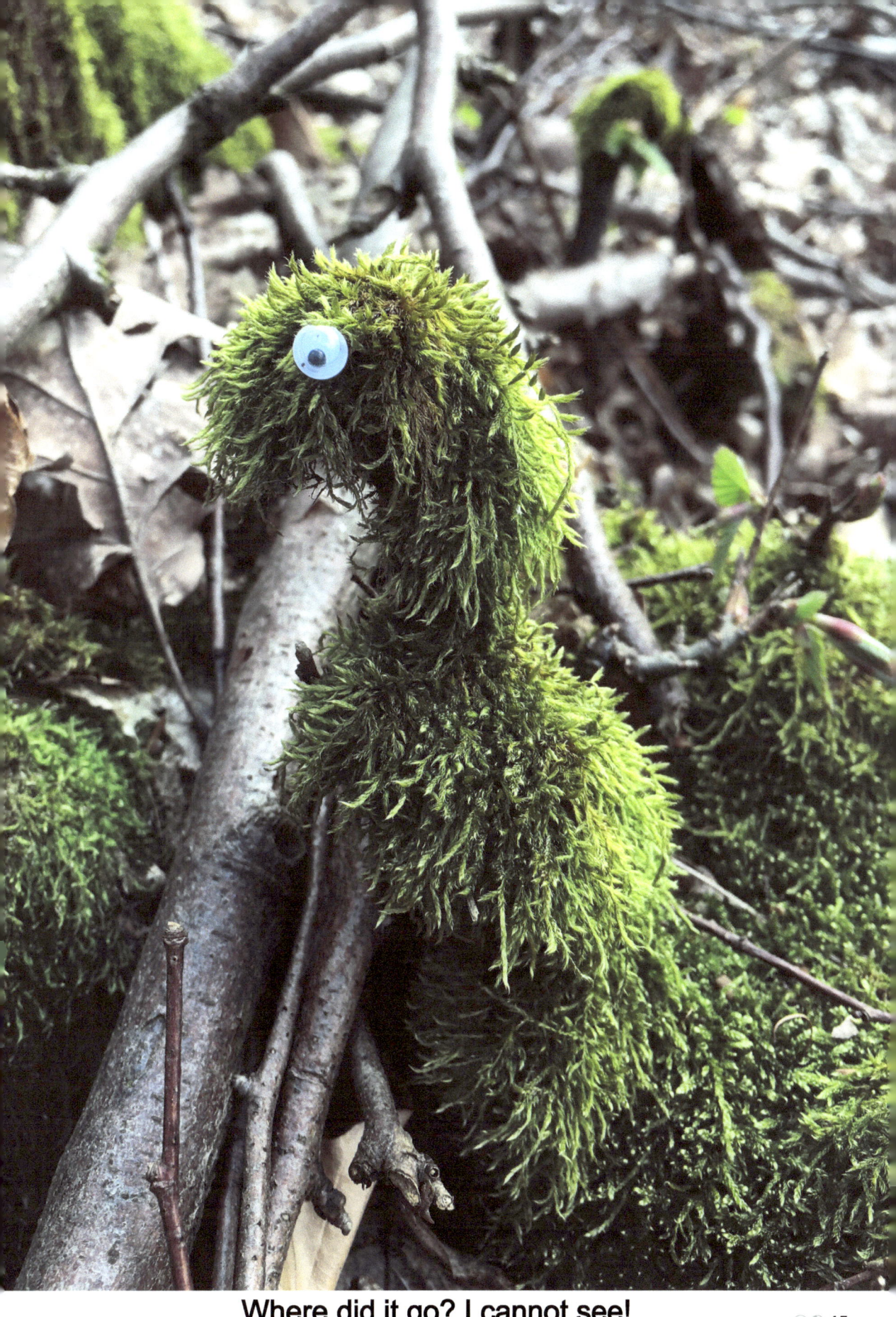

Where did it go? I cannot see!

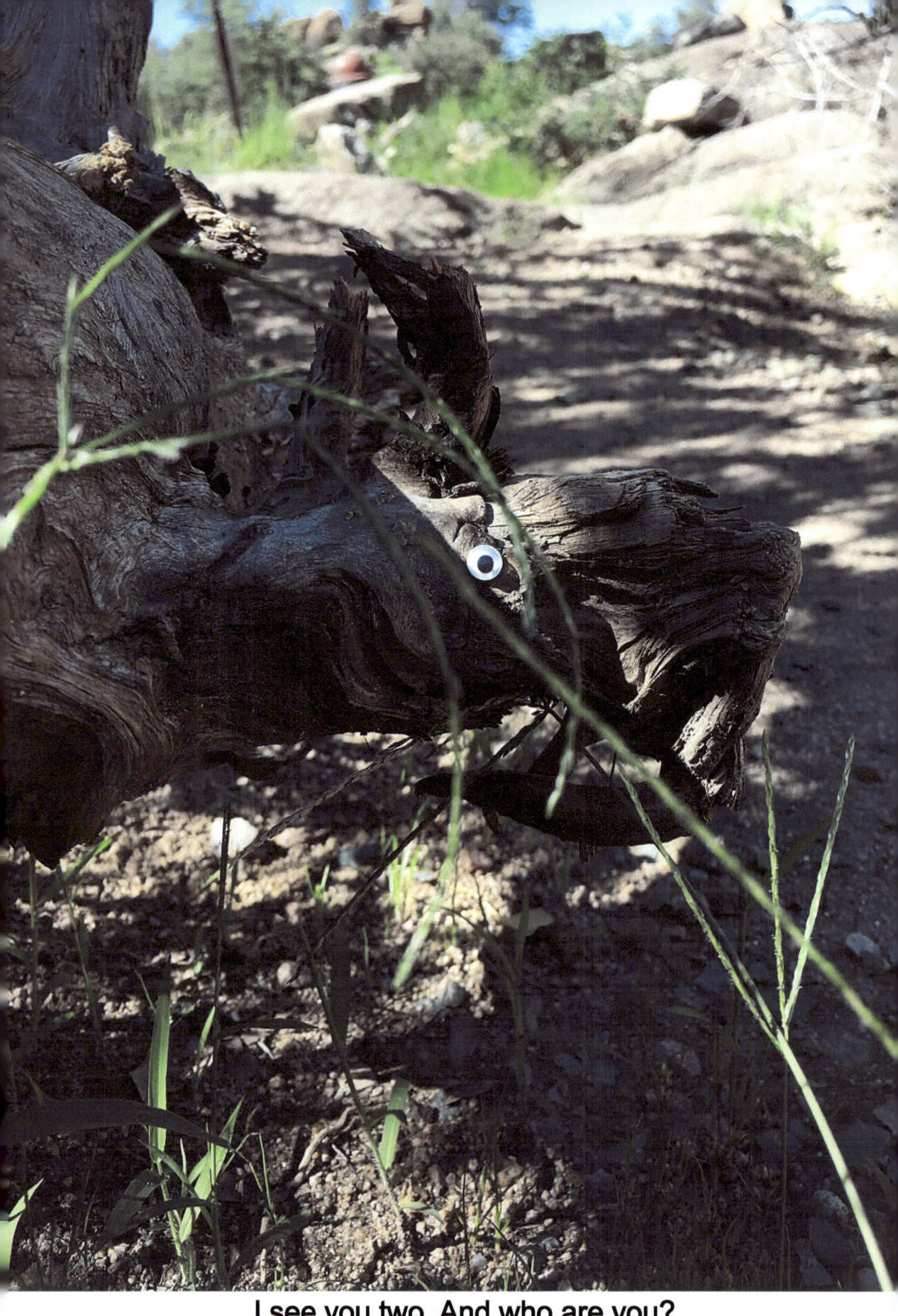

I see you two. And who are you?

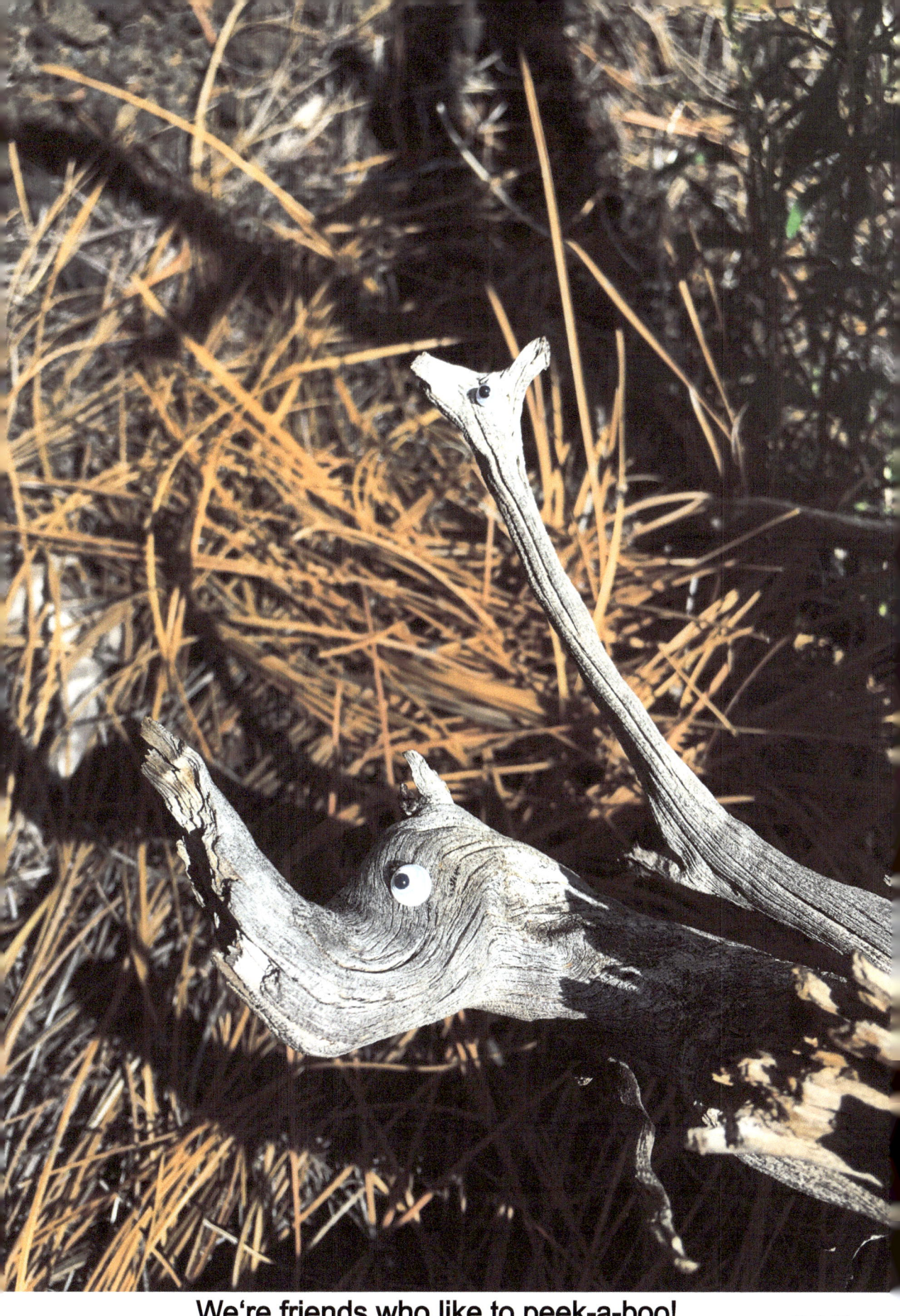

We're friends who like to peek-a-boo!

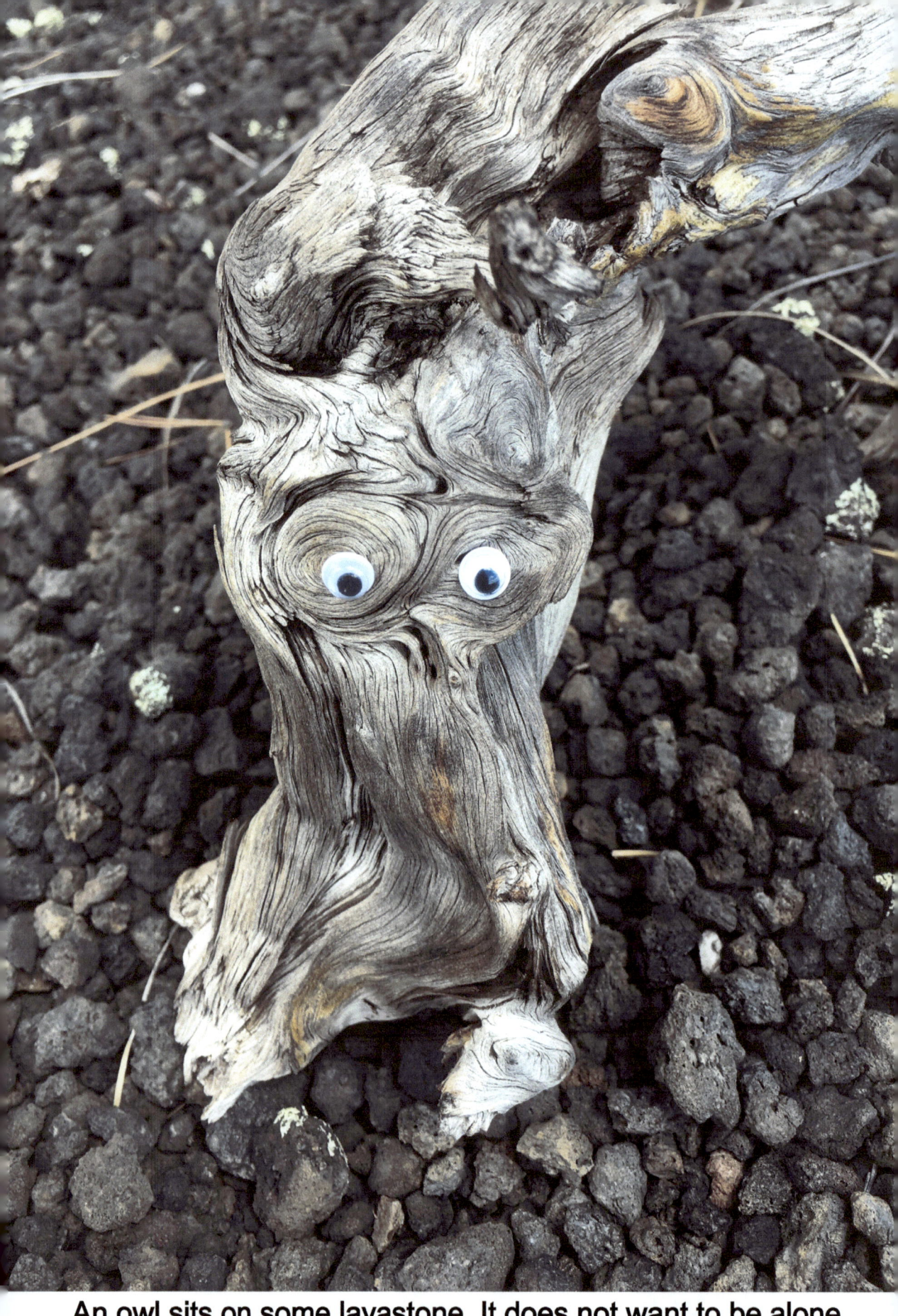
An owl sits on some lavastone. It does not want to be alone.

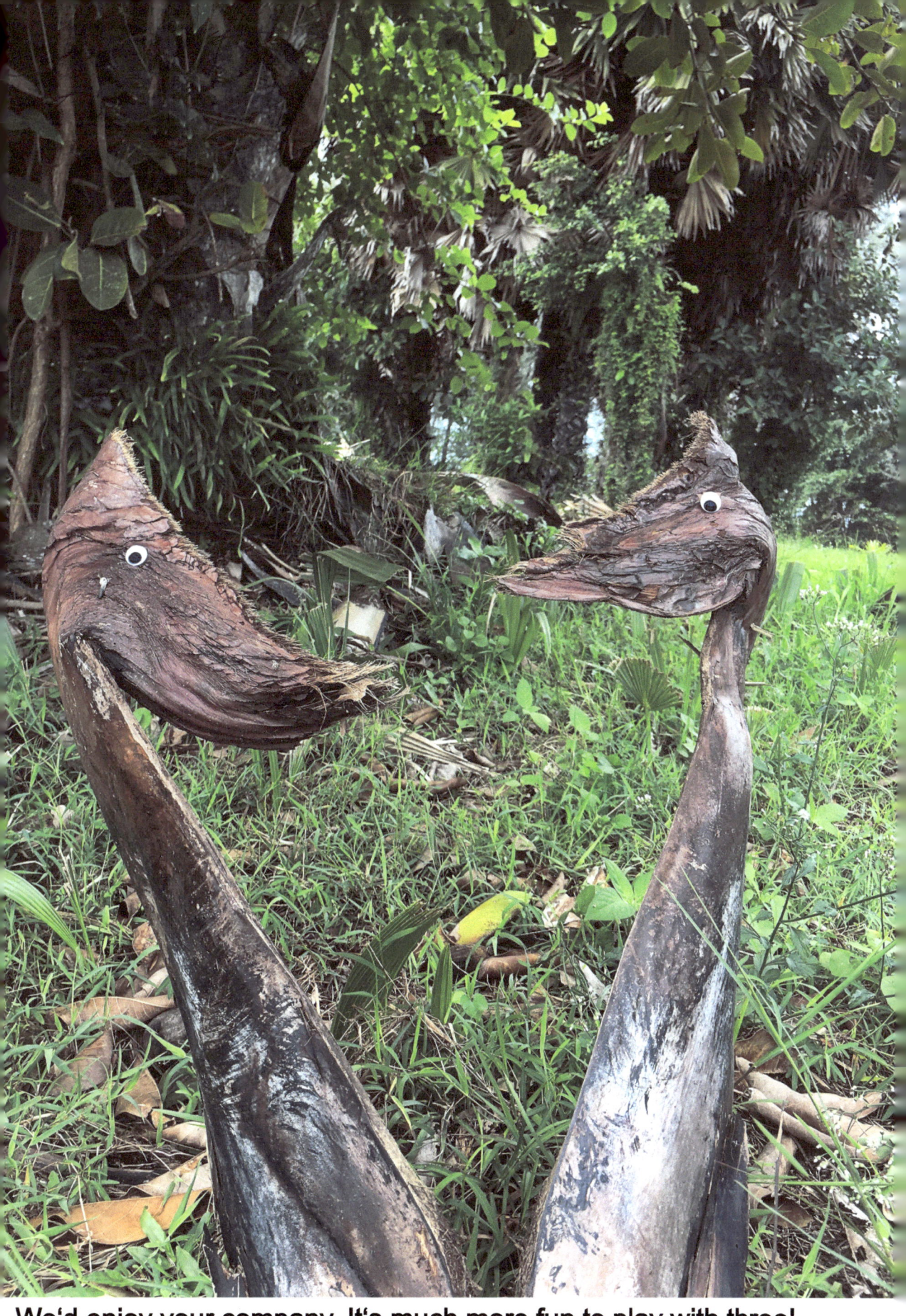
We'd enjoy your company. It's much more fun to play with three!

Oh no.....
This is the last page.

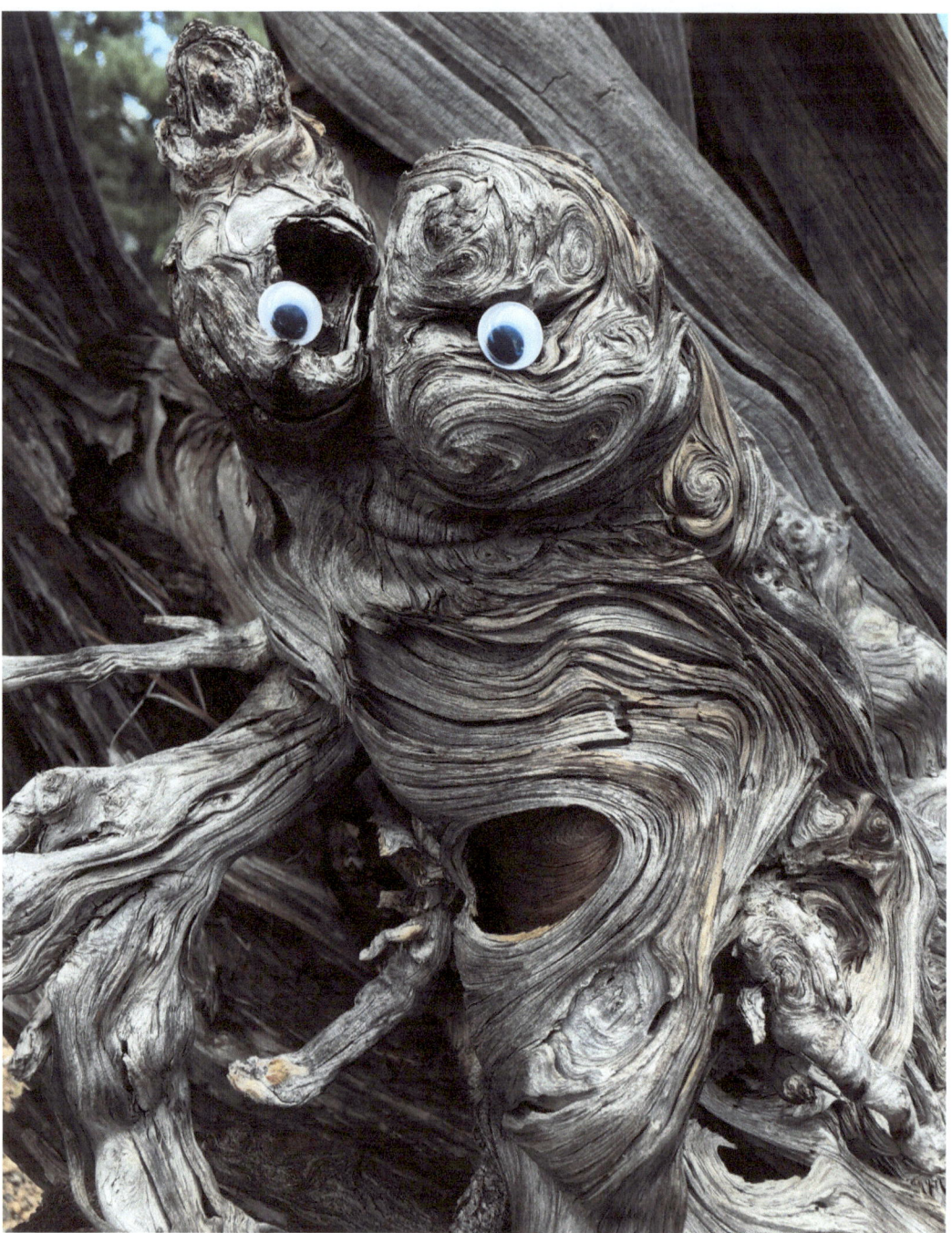

more products at www.mitanderenaugen.eu
more books at amazon and other online or retail stores.

find me on

facebook: www.facebook.com/MitAnderenAugen2016
instagram: www.instagram.com/mitandrenaugen

www.ingramcontent.com/pod-product-compliance
Lightning Source LLC
Chambersburg PA
CBHW051219220526
45473CB00003B/1097